ANTONIO GRAMSCI

D0706109

Is power simply a matter of domination and resistance? Or can a ruling power be vulnerable; can subordinates find their resistance neutralized; and what is the role of culture in this? Gramsci's work invites people to think beyond simplistic oppositions by recasting ideological domination as hegemony: the ability of a ruling power's values to live in the minds and lives of its subalterns as a spontaneous expression of their own interests. Targeting readers encountering Gramsci for the first time, Steve Jones covers key elements of his thought through detailed discussion of:

- culture
- hegemony
- intellectuals
- crisis
- Americanization

In doing so, *Antonio Gramsci* studies the historical context of the theorist's thought, offers examples of putting Gramsci's ideas into practice in the analysis of contemporary culture, and evaluates responses to his work.

Steve Jones is senior lecturer in Media and Cultural Studies at Nottingham Trent University. He teaches and researches in the areas of national identity and material culture and is co-author of *Food and Cultural Studies* (2004).

ROUTLEDGE CRITICAL THINKERS

Series Editor: Robert Eaglestone, Royal Holloway,
University of London

Routledge Critical Thinkers is a series of accessible introductions to key figures in contemporary critical thought.

With a unique focus on historical and intellectual contexts, each volume examines a key theorist's:

- significance
- motivation
- key ideas and their sources
- impact on other thinkers

Concluding with extensively annotated guides to further reading, *Routledge Critical Thinkers* are the student's passport to today's most exciting critical thought.

Already available:

Louis Althusser by Luke Ferretter
Roland Barthes by Graham Allen
Jean Baudrillard by Richard J. Lane
Simone de Beauvoir by Ursula Tidd
Maurice Blanchot by Ullrich Haase
  and William Large
Judith Butler by Sara Salih
Gilles Deleuze by Claire Colebrook
Jacques Derrida by Nicholas Royle
Michel Foucault by Sara Mills
Sigmund Freud by Pamela
  Thurschwell
Stuart Hall by James Procter

Martin Heidegger by Timothy Clark
Fredric Jameson by Adam Roberts
Jean-François Lyotard by Simon
  Malpas
Jacques Lacan by Sean Homer
Julia Kristeva by Noëlle McAfee
Paul de Man by Martin McQuillan
Friedrich Nietzsche by Lee Spinks
Paul Ricoeur by Karl Simms
Edward Said by Bill Ashcroft and Pal
  Ahluwalia
Gayatri Chakravorty Spivak by
  Stephen Morton
Slavoj Žižek by Tony Myers

For further details on this series, see www.routledge.com/literature.

ANTONIO GRAMSCI

Steve Jones

Routledge
Taylor & Francis Group

LONDON AND NEW YORK

First published 2006 by Routledge
2 Park Square, Milton Park, Abingdon, Oxon OX14 4RN

Simultaneously published in the USA and Canada
by Routledge
270 Madison Ave, New York, NY 10016

Reprinted 2007

Routledge is an imprint of the Taylor & Francis Group, an informa business

© 2006 Steve Jones

Typeset in Perpetua by
Keystroke, Jacaranda Lodge, Wolverhampton
Printed and bound in Great Britain by
TJ International Ltd, Padstow, Cornwall

British Library Cataloguing in Publication Data
A catalogue record for this book is available from the British Library

Library of Congress Cataloging in Publication Data
A catalog record for this book has been requested

ISBN10: 0–415–31947–1   ISBN13: 978–0–415–31947–8 (hbk)
ISBN10: 0–415–31948–X   ISBN13: 978–0–415–31948–5 (pbk)
ISBN10: 0–203–62552–8   ISBN13: 978–0–203–62552–1 (ebk)

CONTENTS

Series editor's preface   vii
Acknowledgements   xi

WHY GRAMSCI?   1

KEY IDEAS   11

1   Gramsci's political and intellectual development   13
2   Culture   27
3   Hegemony   41
4   Hegemony in practice 1: identity   57
5   Hegemony in practice 2: representations and institutions   69
6   Intellectuals   81
7   Crisis   95
8   Americanism and Fordism   109

AFTER GRAMSCI   121

FURTHER READING   135

Works cited   141
Index   149

SERIES EDITOR'S PREFACE

The books in this series offer introductions to major critical thinkers who have influenced literary studies and the humanities. The *Routledge Critical Thinkers* series provides the books you can turn to first when a new name or concept appears in your studies.

Each book will equip you to approach a key thinker's original texts by explaining her or his key ideas, putting them into context and, perhaps most importantly, showing you why this thinker is considered to be significant. The emphasis is on concise, clearly written guides which do not presuppose a specialist knowledge. Although the focus is on particular figures, the series stresses that no critical thinker ever existed in a vacuum but, instead, emerged from a broader intellectual, cultural and social history. Finally, these books will act as a bridge between you and the thinker's original texts: not replacing them but rather complementing what she or he wrote.

These books are necessary for a number of reasons. In his 1997 auto-biography, *Not Entitled*, the literary critic Frank Kermode wrote of a time in the 1960s:

> On beautiful summer lawns, young people lay together all night, recovering from their daytime exertions and listening to a troupe of Balinese musicians. Under their blankets or their sleeping bags, they would chat drowsily about the gurus of the time. . . . What they repeated was largely hearsay; hence my lunchtime suggestion, quite impromptu, for a series of short, very

cheap books offering authoritative but intelligible introductions to such figures.

There is still a need for 'authoritative and intelligible introductions'. But this series reflects a different world from the 1960s. New thinkers have emerged and the reputations of others have risen and fallen, as new research has developed. New methodologies and challenging ideas have spread through the arts and humanities. The study of literature is no longer – if it ever was – simply the study and evaluation of poems, novels and plays. It is also the study of the ideas, issues and difficulties which arise in any literary text and in its interpretation. Other arts and humanities subjects have changed in analogous ways.

With these changes, new problems have emerged. The ideas and issues behind these radical changes in the humanities are often presented without reference to wider contexts or as theories which you can simply 'add on' to the texts you read. Certainly, there's nothing wrong with picking out selected ideas or using what comes to hand – indeed, some thinkers have argued that this is, in fact, all we can do. However, it is sometimes forgotten that each new idea comes from the pattern and development of somebody's thought and it is important to study the range and context of their ideas. Against theories 'floating in space', the *Routledge Critical Thinkers* series places key thinkers and their ideas firmly back in their contexts.

More than this, these books reflect the need to go back to the thinker's own texts and ideas. Every interpretation of an idea, even the most seemingly innocent one, offers its own 'spin', implicitly or explicitly. To read only books on a thinker, rather than texts by that thinker, is to deny yourself a chance of making up your own mind. Sometimes what makes a significant figure's work hard to approach is not so much its style or content as the feeling of not knowing where to start. The purpose of these books is to give you a 'way in' by offering an accessible overview of these thinkers' ideas and works and by guiding your further reading, starting with each thinker's own texts. To use a metaphor from the philosopher Ludwig Wittgenstein (1889–1951), these books are ladders, to be thrown away after you have climbed to the next level. Not only, then, do they equip you to approach new ideas, but also they empower you, by leading you back to a theorist's own texts and encouraging you to develop your own informed opinions.

Finally, these books are necessary because, just as intellectual needs have changed, the education systems around the world – the contexts in which introductory books are usually read – have changed radically too. What was suitable for the minority higher education system of the 1960s is not suitable for the larger, wider, more diverse, high technology education systems of the twenty-first century. These changes call not just for new, up-to-date introductions but new methods of presentation. The presentational aspects of *Routledge Critical Thinkers* have been developed with today's students in mind.

Each book in the series has a similar structure. They begin with a section offering an overview of the life and ideas of each thinker and explain why she or he is important. The central section of each book discusses the thinker's key ideas, their context, evolution and reception. Each book concludes with a survey of the thinker's impact, outlining how their ideas have been taken up and developed by others. In addition, there is a detailed final section suggesting and describing books for further reading. This is not a 'tacked-on' section but an integral part of each volume. In the first part of this section you will find brief descriptions of the thinker's key works, then, following this, information on the most useful critical works and, in some cases, on relevant websites. This section will guide you in your reading, enabling you to follow your interests and develop your own projects. Throughout each book, references are given in what is known as the Harvard system (the author and the date of a work cited are given in the text and you can look up the full details in the bibliography at the back). This offers a lot of information in very little space. The books also explain technical terms and use shaded boxes to describe events or ideas in more detail, away from the main emphasis of the discussion. Boxes are also used at times to highlight definitions of terms frequently used or coined by a thinker. In this way, the boxes serve as a kind of glossary, easily identified when flicking through the book.

The thinkers in the series are 'critical' for three reasons. First, they are examined in the light of subjects that involve criticism: principally Literary Studies or English and Cultural Studies, but also other disciplines that rely on the criticism of books, ideas, theories and unquestioned assumptions. Second, they are critical because studying their work will provide you with a 'tool kit' for your own informed critical reading and thought, which will make you critical. Third, these thinkers are critical because they are crucially important: they deal with ideas and questions which can overturn conventional understandings of the world, of texts, of everything we take for granted, leaving us with a deeper understanding of what we already knew and with new ideas.

No introduction can tell you everything. However, by offering a way into critical thinking, this series hopes to begin to engage you in an activity which is productive, constructive and potentially life-changing.

ACKNOWLEDGEMENTS

I would like to thank the following people for their help: Kate Ahl and Katrina Chandler at Routledge, Bob Eaglestone for initiating the project and being a thoughtful editor throughout, and friends and colleagues at Nottingham Trent University.

This book is for Anna Taylor and our son, Billy, and for my mum and dad, June and Derek Jones. To you all, 'a tender hug'.

WHY GRAMSCI?

TALKING COMMON SENSE

Rather than begin this book with a potted explanation of Antonio Gramsci's thought, I want you answer the question 'Why Gramsci?' yourself, by 'doing' some Gramscian analysis, albeit analysis of a cultural form with which Gramsci himself would have been entirely unfamiliar. Take a piece of participatory media (what is sometimes called 'open access' or 'talkback' media – one of the ever-widening range of broadcasts in which panels of experts and members of the public discuss and debate the issues of the day). This could be a website message board, a radio phone-in, a television discussion programme or a news item in which journalists interview members of the public on the street. Your chosen programme might deal with an obviously political issue (foreign policy, say, or the health system), but it will not be a pointless exercise if it deals with something that seems more personal or everyday – perhaps a discussion of obesity, a programme about relationships, or a sports phone-in. What I want to suggest is that, despite the heterogeneity of voices taking part in these programmes – their apparent variety and diversity – certain values will be shared amongst the programme makers, the participants and the audience, not least the beliefs that heterogeneous opinion is itself to be applauded, and that the broadcast media provide a neutral forum for its display. I want to suggest further that the ways in which these values are negotiated indicate the *equilibrium* that is constantly being established between different social and political groups.

In particular, I want you to note four features of the programme. First, what is its context? Why is it being broadcast now rather than at some other time? Such programmes are frequently motivated by a newsworthy event, or by a pronouncement made by a prominent figure. Is your chosen text a product of such a recent and singular occurrence, or might there be a broader 'climate' in which it is being transmitted (a heightened sense that parental authority is waning, say, or a feeling that the institution of marriage is in jeopardy)? Second, what constitutes the 'reasonable centre' of the debate, for which there will be a large groundswell of support? Are there common-sense assumptions that go unchallenged (or are enthusiastically supported) by the great majority of the participants? And are there positions within the debate that are noisily silenced, or opinions that are not heard at all? Which wisdoms are used to conclude the debate?

A third thing to look for is the role of experts in your chosen discussion. Does the format allow for a single expert, or does it reproduce the principle of diversity and heterogeneity by offering a number of experts with differing positions on a topic? Does the programme's host have a role in mediating or choosing between these competing positions? Is the host cast in the role of expert him- or herself? Do experts provide a touchstone of authority for the discussion, to which non-experts will always defer? Or are they characterized as out of touch with common sense, and noisily silenced? (During a radio debate on the morning in which I wrote this, a criminologist who argued that crime statistics in the UK do not justify tough new police measures was cast in this unfortunate role.)

Fourth, I want you think about how the debate constructs the meaning of things *spatially*. Does the programme fashion an image of the nation (as, perhaps, being under threat from immigrants, or as a nation of couch potatoes), or is its spatial frame of reference more local (this will, of course, be particularly true of regional programming, but fierce local loyalties may surface in other formats in, say, discussions of sport, work, health or food policy)? What kinds of discussion might lead participants to think beyond these boundaries, to describe themselves as, for example, good Europeans, global citizens, or members of world religions, and do other participants readily accept these identifications?

EXERCISE: Study a piece of participatory media, noting your responses to the various issues raised above. Are there any further issues that the discussion brings into focus?

GRAMSCI'S NUANCED ACCOUNT OF POWER

While we can readily identify the motifs and conventions that typify this kind of programming, the most difficult thing to do is to decide whose interests the debate serves. Does the discussion ultimately reproduce what we might think of as 'dominant' values (you might ask yourself what *are* the dominant values in your society?) or does it challenge them (perhaps you feel that, within your programme, ordinary people invert the normal operations of power by criticizing their social and political superiors)? Perhaps it does neither (you might feel this to be the case in those formats that deal extensively with personal narratives), or both (where apparently opposing values seem to cancel one another out)? Or maybe power lies outside the programme itself, being invested in its researchers and producers, in the broadcast authorities who commission and schedule it and in the goverment that legislates for, scrutinizes and licenses the broadcast media? That there is no simple or single answer to this question is indicated by Sonia Livingstone and Peter Lunt's (1994) study of television talk, in which they suggest that alongside its traditional roles of acting on behalf of, and criticizing, the government, discussion programmes now carry out three further roles:

> They can act as spokesmen for the people to both government and experts, conveying opinions, experiences, information and criticism 'upwards' to the elite. They can allow the public to hold politicians and experts to account directly, rather than by proxy . . . And they can provide a social space for communication among the lay public itself, both in the form of the studio audience and in the relation between studio and home audiences, and thus give everyday experiences and opinions a new and powerful legitimation.
>
> (Livingstone and Lunt 1994: 5)

It is this complex, multi-layered understanding of the web of power that provides an answer to the question 'Why Gramsci?' posed at the beginning of this chapter. Antonio Gramsci (1891–1937) recognized that social power is not a simple matter of domination on the one hand and subordination or resistance on the other. Rather than imposing their will, 'dominant' groups (or, more precisely, dominant alliances, coalitions or blocs) within democratic societies generally govern with a good degree of *consent* from the people they rule, and the maintenance of that consent is dependent upon an incessant repositioning of the relationship between rulers and ruled. In order to maintain its authority, a ruling power must be sufficiently flexible to respond to new circumstances and to the changing wishes of those it rules. It must be able to reach into the minds and lives of its subordinates, exercising its power as what appears to be a free expression of their own interests and desires. In the process, the ruling coalition will have to take on at least some of the values of those it attempts to lead, thereby reshaping its own ideals and imperatives.

Because of this incessant activity, Gramsci rejects the notion that power is something that can be achieved once and for all. Instead he conceives of it as an ongoing process, operative even at those moments when a ruling class or group can no longer generate consent. In the process, society becomes *saturated* with attempts to police the boundary between the desires of the dominant and the demands of the subjugated. Gramsci's highly original understanding of power sees it as something actively lived by the oppressed as a form of common sense (hence my suggestion that you look at a discussion programme, a broadcast form in which common sense is central). As the British cultural theorist Raymond Williams notes, this was a huge advance on those critical positions that assumed that ideologies were simply false ideas imposed upon people. Gramsci's analysis, he writes:

> supposes the existence of something which is truly total . . . but which is lived at such a depth, which saturates society to such an extent, and which even constitutes the substance and limit of common sense for most people under its sway, that it corresponds to the reality of [their] social experience . . . If ideology were merely some abstract, imposed set of notions, if our social and political and cultural ideas and assumptions and habits were merely the result of specific manipulation, of a kind of overt training which might be simply ended or withdrawn, then the society would be very much easier to move and to change than in practice it has ever been or is.
>
> (Williams 1980: 37)

This negotiation between groups takes place in many spheres (for example, in parliament, in the family, at work, in schools, universities and hospitals), but as Williams argues, it also takes place within culture, and Gramsci is one of the first Marxist theoreticians to recognize that culture is not simply the expression of underlying economic relations (I shall discuss Marxism in greater detail in Key Idea 2). By distancing cultural criticism from a 'vulgar' overemphasis on economic relations, Gramsci's work opens up the possibility of considering other forms of social and cultural relationship (gender, 'race', sexuality, religion, environmentalism and so on) as matters for analysis in their own right. But, crucially, it does not do so by abandoning the question of class. <u>Major social change which leaves the condition of the working class fundamentally unaltered is, for Gramsci, no change at all.</u>

Instead of seeing the economy as determining culture and politics, Gramsci argues that culture, politics and the economy are organized in a relationship of mutual exchange with one another, a constantly circulating and shifting network of influence. To this process he gives the name *hegemony* and one of the central aims of this book is to show you how hegemony differs fundamentally from domination. Seeing hegemony as a dynamic *process* militates against the view that students of culture can understand the meaning of a text in isolation. In this sense, asking you to analyse a single participatory programme was mildly disingenuous, since no one representation can capture the nexus of power at any one moment – it is indeed, for Gramsci, precisely not something that one can pin down since it is always 'in the process of becoming' (1995: 312). Nor is the study of texts and images a pointless task, since as Colin Mercer observes, 'when we begin to consider the *relationships* between images, their combined effects and modes of persuasion, then we are getting closer to the question at hand' (Mercer 1984: 5).

To this, we could also add the need to consider the relationships between the images themselves and the variety of cultural institutions that are active in any historical period. Gramscian analysis directs us away from a preoccupation with the text alone and towards an understanding that texts are bound up with the agencies involved in cultural production, some of which act in concert with one another, while others act in competition. A full account of a film, for example, would include some address to the film studio that produced it, and to the roles of censorship, film criticism and popular taste in the period. Consideration of a newspaper article would reflect on the patterns of ownership at that moment, the composition of the reading public, the role of government in licensing the press and the activities of industry watchdogs. In the next section, I outline a brief case study, showing how this web of power and meaning coheres around a single media event, and how this may be related to Gramsci's major theoretical concerns.

CASE STUDY: ST GEORGE'S DAY

My chosen example of a participatory media event is the variety of radio, television and web events organized by the British Broadcasting Corporation (BBC) in April 2004 to discuss the contemporary meanings of St George's Day, the festival commemorating the English patron saint and, by extension,

English identity and history. 'Festival', here, may be somewhat misleading, since relatively few English people celebrate the day (or even know precisely when it is), and the English are not given a holiday every 23 April. Indeed, one of the motivations for the BBC's coverage was a growing sense that St George's Day should be made an official public holiday, a sentiment articulated by Tom Watson, a Labour Member of Parliament. Mr Watson proposed a motion calling on the government to make St George's Day a 'national day of celebration' and commended his local council, Sandwell, for organizing a pageant of Englishness. But the terms in which this speech was made suggested the climate of concern that surrounded the event. Arguing for the observance of St George's Day meant dealing with two associated phenomena: first, the devolution of centralized (London-based) government to national assemblies in Wales, Scotland and Northern Ireland, and second the gains made in local government in England by the fascist British National Party (BNP).

In dealing with the first issue, Mr Watson made the case that the other nations of the United Kingdom had a more confident relationship with their national symbols. To celebrate St George's Day was simply to bring England in line with its more mature national partners. In Scotland and Wales, he argued 'local symbols like the thistle are now routinely used by political parties. But in England we remain suspicious of such symbols. I'm arguing that we shouldn't be ashamed of the flag of St George' (Moss 2004: 7). Mr Watson's argument therefore begs the question, why *should* the English be afraid of their flag?

An answer to this lies in the attempt to dissociate St George's Day from the BNP. A year earlier, the BNP had participated in an unregulated commemorative march through Sandwell. By turning the march into a licensed event, the council were hoping to marginalize the BNP, which did indeed boycott it. Sandwell Council therefore set up an opposition between the mainstream event and its unofficial predecessor. Translating this into a description of the kind of people willing to participate in a St George's Day march, the mayor of Sandwell offered the opinion that 'the far right has sought to promote the flag and the idea of Englishness as their property rather than that of ordinary, decent people . . . We [however] are seeking to celebrate St George's Day in a non-racist, non-confrontational inclusive way' (ibid.) 'Inclusiveness' here is a shorthand for the non-white population, since the mayor is implicitly acknowledging that widely in the past, and to a lesser extent in the present, describing oneself as English, and celebrating England's national symbols, were the unique rights of white people.

The mayor's point performs a neat rhetorical trick: it translates one version of 'Us' (we, the white English people) into another (we, the ordinary, decent, multi-ethnic English people). It is an attempt to undermine the BNP through showing that its attempt to speak on behalf of Englishness is drastically partial and marginal. In its attempt to shift the ground of Englishness, the piece of rhetoric can be illuminated through the Gramscian concept of the *national-popular*. For Gramsci, one of the key elements of any hegemonic strategy is the formation of links with existing elements of culture, in this case a growing identification by English people with their national symbols. To do otherwise, to reject an embedded culture and impose something entirely new, would point to a division between the culture of the people and their political representatives. When such divisions become unbridgeable they are expressed as a *crisis*. This dangerous situation leaves the ground open for other forces (in this case the BNP) that are better positioned to 'make other arrangements' as the representatives of popular interests. Gramsci is aware that such a task is not without risks. The 'moral and intellectual world' of the people may well be 'backward and conventional' in some ways and the task of a progressive politics is to carefully distinguish between the reactionary features of popular consciousness and the progressive potential that it also contains. The organization of a St George's Day parade that celebrates diversity is clearly an attempt to endorse an English tradition of tolerance while rejecting reactionary, racist strands within the national culture.

To be effective, such ideas need to be embedded through cultural institutions and practices that appear to be independent of politics. Gramsci groups these phenomena under the heading of *civil society*. One of the more lasting and influential institutions of British civil society is the BBC, and its website (BBC 2004a; 2004b) continually replayed the mayor of Sandwell's themes of ordinariness and decency in postings about what it means to be English. There was widespread agreement that being English was incompatible with virulent hostility towards immigrants. A typical example noted that, 'For the record I am white, born in Kent and proud to be English – tradition is important but immigration should not be considered negative *per se*.' Similarly, a number of respondents picked up on the idea that England has a long history of immigration: 'Don't blame immigrants. This island nation has always been cosmopolitan; Romans, Vikings, Normans, Saxons, Indians, Afro-Caribbeans, the list goes on'; 'A true Englishman is a mongrel by the nature of our origins therefore we should celebrate the diversity of our culture' and 'Being English means being part of THE most integrated culturally diverse country on the planet.' Postings repeatedly mentioned the fact that many English people celebrate the Irish national day, St Patrick's Day, as evidence of their reasonableness ('everyone knows about St Paddy's day – fair play to them, they should celebrate'; 'As a Londoner I thoroughly enjoyed the festivities for Chinese New Year and the St Patrick's Day parade'). Given the long history of violent conflict between the English and Irish, such a willingness to enjoy someone else's festivities demonstrated the cherished English sense of fair play. And equally, to celebrate the English national day would simply be 'fair'.

Such reasonableness, however, was haunted by two spectres. A short spell of living in England will suggest to any observer that the English are not noticeably fairer or more tolerant than many other nationalities (which is not to say that they are universally unfair or intolerant). A common refrain in British participatory media is that England is being swamped by large numbers of incomers, many of whom take advantage of innate English generosity. However, to acknowledge that the English are intolerant was not sustainable within the image of national decency that the BBC's respondents were expounding. Intolerance was therefore projected onto another mythical figure, the hooligan, who represents the negative standard against which decency and fairness can be measured. In a number of postings, this intoler- ance was closely associated with questions of class. One writer argued that patriotism is 'associated with our "hooligan" antics in football, and tends to celebrate a more superficial England as opposed to an intellectually and culturally diverse one'. Others felt that 'for years the powers that be have allowed the yobs to own the English flag' and that 'the image of a strongly patriotic English person, sadly often is one of a beer-bellied football hooligan'. Like the mayor of Sandwell's vision of inclusivity, therefore, the construction of a national 'Us' was predicated on the denigration of a loutish, racist 'Them'.

Even more prominent than the shadow of racism, however, was the issue of political correctness (PC). If fascist thugs provided a highly specific image of otherness, the nature and whereabouts of PC was more imprecise – it could be all politicians ('the politicians would have us believe that all such celebrations are nationalist, racist and politically incorrect'); specific politicians ('in his [London Mayor Ken Livingstone's] efforts to be PC he has forgotten that English-born Londoners are also proud of their heritage'); civil servants ('Don't let the politically correct bureaucrats make you feel ashamed to be English'); or simply endemic ('Today England is scared and too politically correct to celebrate itself'). For some respondents, it was precisely the excesses of PC that granted licence to the behaviour of thugs at the opposite end of the political spectrum ('For years the powers that be have allowed the racists and yobs to own the English flag by bending to pressure from the "anti-English" lobbyists'). PC therefore provided a persuasive, if unspecific (persuasive *because* unspecific), focus for people's dissatisfactions with the British state.

These somewhat arbitrary and contradictory motifs – tolerance, decency, the rejection of hooliganism, and the spectre of PC – form the ground of what Gramsci would describe as *common sense*. For Gramsci, common sense is a confused formation, in part drawn from 'official' conceptions of the world circulated by the ruling bloc, in part formed out of people's practical experiences of social life. Despite this unevenness, it offers a deeply held guide to life, directing people to act in certain ways and ruling out other modes of behaviour as unthinkable. Yet Gramsci argues that this is not inevitable. Official and practical conceptions can be dismantled in order to show how they serve the interests of a ruling power. Football hooligans are undoubtedly real, but they are also constructed through media representations of lawless youth and through British politicians' need to demonstrate toughness. Such *moral panics* are a recurrent cultural theme in Britain and elsewhere. Moreover, Gramsci contends that the progressive elements of common sense, what he calls 'good sense', may be teased out of common sense to form the basis of a progressive politics. Thus, while we might be persuaded – with some justification – that hostility to PC is a coded and conspiratorial version of racism, people's resentments were often expressed through criticism of an impersonal bureaucracy. This antagonism could be seized and made transformative, though Gramsci is no utopian: it could equally be channelled into reformism or reaction.

While for the most part, the BBC organized the event as a kind of snapshot of popular attitudes, various experts were on hand to frame the debate in different ways. The BBC London website carried opinion pieces by three commentators: the organizer of the capital's celebrations, who argued that a celebration of Englishness was needed because the English had been 'deculturized' (not least by their own suspicions of rampant nationalism); a journalist from the *Irish Post* who felt that the festivities were 'a self-congratulatory event' that ignored the country's minorities; and a British-Australian writer who offered a visionary list of representative English sights and sounds. Meanwhile, on the news channel Five Live, a historian, responding to various text messages from listeners, offered the opinion that the most prominent characteristic of the English was their self-deprecating humour.

The presence of such figures suggests the emphasis within Gramsci's work on the role of *intellectuals*. While he acknowledges that all people are intellectuals, Gramsci famously makes the point that only some people have the status and function of intellectuals. In his revolutionary conception of society, a new body of 'organic' intellectuals, emerging from a rising class, would work to tease out those progressive elements contained within that class's common sense. Set against this activist figure is the 'traditional' intellectual, once organic to a rising class, but now a marginal figure, divorced from any pressing social reality. While the boundaries of the classes may have shifted, the role of intellectuals as key cultural intermediaries has not. Not only do the website and studio experts give voice to certain currents that are otherwise disorganized, but the network controllers, programme producers and website designers are themselves new forms of intellectual within the greatly expanded sphere of the communications industries.

The issues I have highlighted structure the rest of this book. Key Idea 2 considers the question of culture, its significance within the Marxist tradition, and Gramsci's theorizations of civil society and nation. It provides the foundation for Key Ideas 3, 4 and 5, which analyse Gramsci's theory of hegemony and discuss how it may be applied to various cultural artefacts, institutions and practices. Key Idea 6 examines the role of intellectuals in the hegemonic process, while Key Idea 7 examines Gramsci's notion of crisis. Key Idea 8 covers an issue implicit in any study of European national identity: the impact on economic and cultural life of 'Americanization'. In the final chapter we consider how Gramsci's work has been used and reshaped by later thinkers. In the next chapter, however, we consider another case study of political power and individual agency: that of Antonio Gramsci's life.

SUMMARY

This introduction has argued that Gramsci's major contribution to knowledge is to challenge a simplistic opposition between domination and subordination or resistance. Instead he recasts ideological domination as hegemony: the process of transaction, negotiation and compromise that takes place between ruling and subaltern groups. The chapter has identified the ideas of national-popular, common sense, civil society, crisis and the formation of intellectuals as central to this process of hegemonization. Subsequent chapters will develop these themes and set Gramsci's thought within broader intellectual, aesthetic and political currents.

KEY IDEAS

1

GRAMSCI'S POLITICAL AND INTELLECTUAL DEVELOPMENT

For the most part this book will argue that Gramsci's theories are relevant to the study of contemporary culture. However, you might reasonably ask whether it is not anachronistic to use the work of an early-twentieth-century Marxist to analyse modern cultural forms and practices. Many of the categories that are central to Gramsci's analysis ('proletariat', 'peasantry', 'folklore', 'Fordism') are less prominent or clearly defined than in his lifetime, and some of his observations on popular culture (for example on jazz and football) turned out to be very wide of the mark. Perhaps it is the case that his explanatory frameworks are equally specific to their period, and consequently outmoded? Later chapters will address the question of why, and how, we may use Gramsci's work outside its historical and geographical 'moment', but let us for now observe that Gramsci himself lends some support to such scepticism, for he forcefully draws our attention to the necessity of studying events, ideas, texts and behaviour within their historical context. As a consequence of this, he saw placing one's own life within a political and intellectual context as one of the most pressing philosophical activities. 'The starting-point of critical elaboration', he writes, 'is . . . "knowing thyself" as a product of the historical process to date which has deposited in you an infinity of traces' (1971: 324).

This chapter therefore places Gramsci's thought within a historical framework, mapping out the 'infinity of traces' that led to its formation. On the one hand, this is a grand narrative of political and intellectual change, setting the development of Gramsci's ideas within the context of wider political developments in Italy and Europe during the late nineteenth and early twentieth centuries. But as Gramsci would have been aware, such broad changes could not entirely *determine* his theoretical evolution: he was not simply the effect of other people's writings but also an agent in his own intellectual construction. Understanding the development of his thought is therefore a means of comprehending the interplay of impersonal structures, human agency and chance occurrence (or contingency) in any intellectual and cultural formation.

RISORGIMENTO AND *TRASFORMISMO*

The Italy that Gramsci was born into, in 1891, was a new nation. Until 1861, Italy was a patchwork of provinces ruled by an assortment of traditional monarchs and foreign powers. While small parts of the country developed a modern, industrial infrastructure, much of it consisted of large estates, on which an impoverished peasantry scraped a subsistence-level existence. As was the case in a number of European and South American countries during the nineteenth century, this backwardness led a significant minority of middle-class and aristocratic activists to agitate for national self-determination. Although local uprisings could act as the catalyst for action, at no stage did this desire for independence translate into a mass uprising of the Italian people. Instead, self-rule came piecemeal, through three wars of unification known collectively as the *Risorgimento* ('the Resurgence').

The Risorgimento was directed by an uneasy confederation of two Italian parties: the Moderates, led by the liberal Count Camillo Cavour (1810–61), chief minister of the northern kingdom of Piedmont, and the republican Action Party, led initially by Giuseppe Mazzini and later by Giuseppe Garibaldi (1807–82). The latter played an important role in one of the most significant events of the Risorgimento, the liberation of Sicily and Naples from Spanish Bourbon rule. Alarmed by Garibaldi's autonomous action, Cavour dispatched a Piedmontese army southwards, their union with Garibaldi's force leading to the formal declaration of Italian unification in 1861. However, once Italy had established a parliamentary democracy, the policies of the 'right-wing' Moderates and 'left-wing' Action Party were largely identical, with both parties committed to a programme of industrial modernization, political reform and imperial expansion. Over time, Italy became governed by a variety of Left–Right coalitions in a period known as the *Trasformismo*, after the policy of 'transforming' the party conflicts of the Risorgimento into a centrist consensus.

Gramsci saw the Risorgimento and its aftermath as a key example of how a governing power absorbs its political antagonists and institutes reform, without expanding its programme to involve full democratic participation. He argued that the Moderate Party was successful because it represented a specific class. The intellectuals who made up its leadership were drawn from the class of estate owners and northern industrialists whose interests they served – in Gramsci's term they were 'condensed'. By contrast, the Action Party was not organically connected to any particular class (instead it adopted a paternalistic attitude to the popular classes, particularly the peasantry) and could not therefore develop a condensed political programme. Action Party policies were often marked by their inconsistency around, for example, hostility to the Church, or land reform, inconsistencies which ultimately failed the peasantry in whose name they presumed to speak. In this situation, writes Gramsci, the Action Party became a subaltern party to the Moderates. This does not mean that it was defeated – rather it became a junior partner in an alliance, actively identifying with the aims of the Moderates and adopting Moderate values as its own. In a famous passage, Gramsci observes that:

> A social group *dominates* antagonistic groups, which it tends to 'liquidate', or to subjugate perhaps even by armed force; it *leads* kindred and allied groups. A social group can, and indeed must, already exercise 'leadership' before winning governmental power (this indeed is one of the principal conditions for the winning of such power); it subsequently becomes dominant when it exercises power, but even if it holds it firmly in its grasp it must continue to 'lead' as well.
>
> (Gramsci 1971: 57–8; emphasis added)

It is from this perspective that Gramsci observes that the whole history of the Italian state from 1848 to the 1920s can be characterized as one of *trasformismo*, initially a 'molecular' transformism as individuals passed into the conservative camp, and later a transformism of whole groups, as leftist radicals became supporters first of imperialism and subsequently of Italian intervention into the First World War. While these adventures appeared to have a popular and national dimension to them, they were actually deeply inimical to the interests of the working class and agricultural labour.

EARLY LIFE

The Risorgimento and the period of *trasformismo* impacted directly upon Antonio Gramsci's early life. He was born in the town of Ales on the island of Sardinia where his father, Francesco, worked as a land registrar. Although prior to unification Sardinia was part of the northern kingdom that included Piedmont, the island was more typical of the *Mezzogiorno* (Southern Italy) with a rudimentary agrarian economy that had been devastated by a series of banking and export crises. As a middle-ranking state servant, Francesco, his wife Giuseppina, and their seven children were initially relatively immune to this poverty. This changed, however, when Francesco aligned himself with an unsuccessful parliamentary candidate in the 1897 elections. Corruption and local vendettas played a major role in Sardinian politics and Francesco laid himself open to reprisal. He was convicted of embezzlement and sentenced to five and a half years in prison. Without his salary, the Gramsci family was reduced to a state of near-destitution. Despite Antonio being a promising pupil, he was taken out of school at the age of 11.

This was not Antonio's only misfortune. When he was 3 he contracted a spinal problem, leaving him permanently hunchbacked and abnormally short (his illness was probably rickets, though the Gramsci family claimed that a clumsy nursemaid had dropped him down the stairs). Despite some primitive and agonizing attempts to correct his disability, severe ill-health would dog Gramsci for the rest of his life. 'The doctors', he later wrote, 'had given me up for dead, and until about 1914 my mother kept the small coffin and little dress I was supposed to be buried in' (Fiori 1970: 17). His sickliness, the visibility of his deformity and his suddenly reduced class status left Gramsci particularly vulnerable to the harshness of village life (Davidson 1977: 27), as a consequence of which he became intensely withdrawn. This aspect of his personality would resurface at regular intervals throughout his life. Years later Gramsci described himself as like a 'worm inside a cocoon, unable to unwind himself' (1979: 263).

Francesco Gramsci was eventually released from prison and the family's financial conditions improved sufficiently to send Antonio back to school. At the age of 17 Gramsci moved with his older brother Gennaro to Cagliari, the capital of the island, to enrol at the *liceo*, or grammar school. Despite severe poverty (letters home recounted how he could not go to school because he had no serviceable clothes and shoes), Gramsci won a scholarship to the University of Turin, enrolling on the Modern Philosophy course in 1911.

These personal developments took place against the background of changing events in Sardinia, which would influence Gramsci's politics and thought in competing directions. Another agricultural slump provoked the development of rudimentary industry in the form of foreign-owned mines. When the miners, who lived and worked in conditions of incredible squalor, went on strike at Bugerru, three were shot dead. The killings provoked a general strike in Italy, and the development of a more politicized consciousness amongst islanders of all classes. This related not only to the events at Bugerru, but more broadly to the treatment of the *Mezzogiorno* by the government of the day, whose concessions to northern industrialists and the organized working-class movement tended to further impoverish the rural South, in turn generating a sense of inter-regional and intra-class animosity. Mass rioting in Cagliari in 1906 led to hundreds of arrests, with troops firing into unarmed crowds.

As a consequence of this militancy and its subjugation, there was a well-developed infrastructure for protest in Cagliari by the time Gramsci arrived. Gennaro was secretary of the local Socialist Party, and Gramsci was befriended by a teacher, Raffa Garzia, who commissioned articles from his student for a Sardist (Sardinian nationalist) newspaper. Gramsci was also influenced by a radical socialist, Gaetano Salvemini, who argued against the exploitation of the *Mezzogiorno* by the North, and demanded that the southern peasantry be given the vote (although illiteracy was endemic in the South, illiterate Italian men were disqualified from voting. Italian women were not enfranchised until 1945). It was, therefore, as a young radical divided between international socialism and Sardist exceptionalism that Gramsci sailed for Turin in 1911.

'YEARS OF IRON AND FIRE': GRAMSCI IN TURIN

Gramsci's student years were dominated by a continual battle with his physical limitations, exacerbated by the lack of adequate financial support from his family. In one letter home, he recounts a 'glacial existence' in which he would walk around Turin 'shivering with cold, then come back to a cold room and sit shivering for hours' (Fiori 1970: 73). Compounding this hand-to-mouth existence was the need to achieve academic success in order to retain his university scholarship. After a series of physical and nervous breakdowns, however, he was forced to abandon his degree course in April 1915.

Despite this, 1911–15 were years of intellectual evolution for Gramsci as he came to embrace socialism and reject his early Sardism. He never, however, abandoned the notion that the South was effectively colonized by the North. This transition was given urgency by working-class militancy in Turin, but it was also a struggle carried out in ideas. Gramsci arrived at university at a time when Italian (and indeed European) intellectual life was being influenced by a strong current of *anti-positivism* – a reaction against the idea that social life could be studied using the same 'objective' laws as natural science. Furthermore, as Lynne Lawner argues, although the currents of thought composing positivism took a number of forms, they shared 'a set of political views that can be defined as reformist or gradualist' (Lawner 1979: 17). While this involved welcome developments in education and health, it also advanced the notion that different strata of Italian society (the 'elite' and 'the masses'), and different regions of the country (the North and the South), had reached different levels of development and therefore possessed separate cultures. From Gramsci's perspective, this was compounded by a positivist tendency to cement together the economically privileged sectors of society (the relatively wealthy industrial working class, the middle class and the southern landowners) as the assumed representatives of an evolving, modernizing Italy. For the later Gramsci, the Socialist Party itself contributed to this ideology, assembling a northern alliance that defined itself against the 'ball and chain' of southern backwardness. Thus, Gramsci's disavowal of Sardism was not a withdrawal from the 'Southern Question'. Instead he engaged in a critique of the 'sociologists of positivism' who gave intellectual support to the development of the 'two cultures'. This divide-and-rule strategy, he claimed, simply perpetuated the rule of the middle class or bourgeoisie by preventing the social development of the whole of Italy.

Gramsci's persistent interest in his homeland was stimulated by contact with the socio-linguist Matteo Bartoli, who encouraged him to work on the Sardinian dialect. He also formed a friendship with the Dante scholar Umberto Cosmo, but his intellectual enthusiasms mostly came from philosophy. In particular, Gramsci encountered the work of Karl Marx (1818–83; see the next chapter) and Bendetto Croce (1866–1952; see box, pp. 19–20). Despite his unsociable personality, he also came into contact with a number of student activists. Angelo Tasca, Umberto Terracini and Gramsci's fellow Sardinian Palmiro Togliatti (1893–1964) were members of the Socialist Youth Organization (Gramsci joined the PSI – the Italian Socialist Party – around 1914) and would be his colleagues in journalism and in the foundation of the Italian Communist Party.

nt 23yrs q age

BENEDETTO CROCE

Gramsci's intellectual formation drew on a number of Italian thinkers. Alongside the writings of Marx and Lenin, the Italian philosophers Niccolò Machiavelli, Antonio Labriola, Giovanni Gentile and, most significantly, Benedetto Croce provided important points of engagement and departure. Croce (1866–1952) was Italy's major intellectual figure for over half a century, a leading southern landowner and liberal senator in the Italian parliament. Initially he was an apologist for fascism, though later he became a prominent critic of Mussolini. Croce's philosophy is *idealist*, in its assertion that external reality is created by 'man's' perceptions of it, and it is therefore anti-positivist since it rejects the notion that thought can only be based on observable phenomena. Within his philosophy, Croce advocated a position of 'idealist realism' in which men and women are ceaselessly required to think a new 'ethical-political' reality, which is implemented through their actions. Since idealist realism gave a role to human perception and agency, it provided a humanist corrective to 'metaphysical' accounts of history, in which a providential destiny shapes the future, and to the crude versions of Marxism in circulation at the time, in which history would be determined simply by developments within the economy. For adopting these positions, and advocating a rejuvenated national culture, Gramsci has been described as 'Crocean'. Croce himself would describe Gramsci as 'one of us'.

Yet for all its professed commitment to a human-centred view of history, Croce's work is open to the charge that it, too, is deeply metaphysical. Rather than dealing with the socially situated struggles of real men and women, Croce advances the notion that there is an abstract essence, or Spirit, guiding history. 'All history', he remarked, 'is the history of Spirit.' For Gramsci, this account of Spirit betrayed Croce's class position and his political orientation. Since Spirit was permanently operative (and for Croce – despite much evidence to the contrary – generally benign and rational), it released people from the requirement to struggle for change on a practical, political level and was therefore depoliticizing and reactionary. Moreover, Spirit was not the property of all people but of a class of liberal intellectuals who were able to elaborate their historical vision into cultural, political and economic forms. By naturalizing and universalizing a highly particular mode of thought and set of political actions, idealist realism thus intellectually underpinned the actually existing form of society in early-twentieth-century Italy. For Gramsci, Croce therefore hovers uneasily between the positions of organic intellectual in the service of the emergent liberal bourgeoisie and traditional intellectual, rendered anachronistic by the rise of mass political movements. (For more on Croce, see Bellamy 1987.)

WAR, FASCISM AND COMMUNISM

Gramsci's period in Turin coincided with an increase in Italian militarism and a drift towards war. Deprived of an overseas empire as a consequence of its late unification, Italy attempted to gain a foothold in North Africa by occupying a number of Libyan ports. Despite the military success of this colonial adventure, the episode polarized Italian opinion, particularly dividing the Left. This polarization was magnified two years later when Italy was forced to choose whether to enter the First World War. While the Right supported intervention as a means of taking territory from Austria, the Left was split between an 'absolute neutrality' faction and a growing number of interventionists, including Benito Mussolini (1883–1945), the editor of the party's newspaper *Avanti!*.

The pro-war faction prevailed, and Italy entered the war on the side of France, Britain and Russia, only to experience a series of military setbacks, culminating in a disastrous defeat by German forces at Caporetto in 1917. Although Italy ended the First World War by making territorial gains, these were insufficient to disguise the political and economic crisis that the war had engendered. The years immediately after the conflict saw a huge growth in radicalism as inflation and unemployment rose steeply, and workers, peasants, and former soldiers looked towards political organizations for leadership (Ransome 1992: 77–8). While initially these were the established Catholic and socialist groupings, from 1919 a new political force emerged giving expression to the demands of militant nationalists and the lower middle class. Expanding from its base in Milan, Mussolini's Fascist Party had, by 1921, taken control of large areas of northern and central Italy.

The growth of the working-class movement and the emergence of the Fascists need to be put in the contexts of events that were occurring outside

Italy, but which had far-reaching effects within Italian politics and society. In Russia, the military and economic pressures of the war provoked a much more intense political crisis than was the case amongst the other fighting powers. With the army in retreat, mass strikes broke out in Russian cities, particularly in the capital, St Petersburg, where, in February 1917, a committee of 'soviets' (workers' councils) and soldiers took control of the city. While the new government was initially reformist, a second revolution in October 1917 gave control of the National Assembly and army to the communist Bolshevik faction under the leadership of Lenin (see next chapter). In 1918, the Assembly was dissolved and the Soviet Socialist Republic, the world's first workers' state, was declared. While this marked a high point for revolutionary socialism, subsequent insurgencies failed to make further gains. Between 1918 and 1920, short-lived socialist revolutions in Germany, Austria and Hungary were suppressed with exceptional brutality.

Towards the end of 1915, Gramsci emerged from the illness that had caused him to give up his university studies. Exempted from military service, he threw himself into political activism, writing cultural and political articles for the socialist journals *Il Grido del Popolo* and *Avanti!* His first article on the Russian Revolution appeared in *Il Grido* in April 1917, where he noted that the mainstream press were characterizing the revolution as a bourgeois one. He, by contrast, was 'persuaded that the Revolution is proletarian in character . . . and will naturally result in a socialist regime' (Fiori 1970: 109). In anti-positivist fashion, he proposed that the Bolshevik Revolution was a revolution 'against Marx's *Capital*', by which he meant the assumption that a workers' revolution could only take place after a bourgeois, capitalist society had been established (Russia in 1917 was still an essentially feudal society, in which the great majority of workers were illiterate peasants). As we shall see, later events would lead him to a more nuanced account of how revolutions are installed and maintained, but he would persist in seeing Lenin as an inspirational revolutionary leader. In some ways this was vindicated by the events of 1917. As news filtered through of the Russian Revolution's success, Italian workers attempted their own insurrection. But deprived of leadership and organization, the revolt was quickly suppressed.

In consequence, Gramsci embarked upon the creation of a new journal entitled *L'Ordine Nuovo* (The New Order). The task of this project, he argued, was to discover 'the Soviet-type traditions of the Italian working class, and [to] lay bare the real revolutionary vein in our history' (Fiori 1970: 118).

He found such a 'Soviet' form of organization in the factory councils that had emerged in Turin, particularly in the Fiat car factories, which dominated the city's industrial life. These organizations, he argued, differed from trade unions in two ways: first because they actually sought to wrest control of production from the capitalists, and second because the factory councils formed a basis for government. In Gramsci's conception elected factory councils, farm councils and district councils would replace bourgeois government, eventually forming the basis of a global system. This, he argued, was democracy from the 'ground up' rather than the 'top down'.

We might note here, with Richard Bellamy (1987: 120), that this somewhat optimistic account of the factory councils begs some important questions: Does it not perpetuate the idea that factory workers are satisfied with industrial labour? How would women fit into this model of democracy? Was Turin unique in having the industrial development necessary for the formation of revolutionary factory councils – why, in particular, did they not develop in the North's other great industrial city, Milan? How were connections to be made with Italy's rural majority? These latter two questions became insistent as the Turinese working class again confronted the factory owners and government in 1920, twice occupying the Fiat factories. This demonstrated that the Factory Councils *could* operate autonomously. However, the strikes lacked support from the rest of Italy and failed to receive leadership from either the PSI or the major Italian trade union confederation. Dismayed by this failure of leadership, Gramsci initially called for a takeover of the PSI by Communists working from within (1994: 196). However, his position was moving increasingly towards a break from the Socialists and the formation of an independent Italian Communist Party (PCI). Yet when this finally came, at Livorno in 1921, Gramsci experienced it as a bitter defeat, for the majority of the working-class movement refused to follow the Communists. 'The Livorno split', he wrote 'was without doubt the greatest single victory won by the reactionary forces' (Fiori 1970: 147).

In the wake of this defeat, fascist violence increased in intensity. As we have seen, fascism gave political expression to the lower middle class. This class felt aggrieved over its 'betrayal' at the end of the war (many of the early Fascists had been soldiers) and hostile towards the aims of the militant working class. The Fascists were certainly willing to act in concert with other middle class groups in combating left-wing militancy, yet to portray them as simply the tools of wealthy industrialists and landowners fails to take into account what was specific and new about Mussolini's party. While Gramsci initially derided them as 'Monkey-people' (Ransome 1992: 97) who 'aped' the higher classes, he later changed his opinion, identifying the existence of 'Two Fascisms', a rural and an urban variant, which he predicted would eventually split (1994: 227–9). This analysis underestimated the Fascists' party organization, and their ability to articulate a political programme that would prove attractive to other sectors of society (such as the Church, conservative groups, monarchists and the army). Aware that his movement was in danger of disintegration, Mussolini organized a 'March on Rome' in October 1922. The king and the elected government's unwillingness to take action against the march led to Mussolini assuming the role of prime minister. Seeking to legally ratify his position, Mussolini called a general election in April 1924. This the Fascists duly won, though they did not achieve complete parliamentary dominance. One elected opposition deputy was Antonio Gramsci.

FROM MOSCOW TO PRISON

The Livorno split did not resolve the crisis of factionalism and in-fighting that bedevilled the Italian Left. While elsewhere in Europe, the Communist International (the Comintern) was arguing for a 'united front', which would ally communism with other progressive parties, the PCI under the leadership of Amadeo Bordiga (1889–1970) persisted with the notion of a 'pure' party, untainted by coalition with non-revolutionary parties. Although ambivalent about this policy, Gramsci was nominated as the PCI's representative on the Comintern's executive committee in Moscow, his period in Russia coinciding with the rise to the leadership of the Russian Communist Party of Josef Stalin (1879–1953).

Again suffering from exhaustion, in 1922 Gramsci was admitted to a sanatorium on the outskirts of the city where he met a violinist, Giulia Schucht. Despite feeling that his appearance made it 'fatally impossible that I should ever be loved', the couple were quickly married. Years later he would argue that without human love, the revolutionary spirit could only be 'a matter of pure intellect, of pure mathematical calculation' (Fiori 1970: 157), yet their relationship would always be fleeting and snatched. It was quickly put to the test when Bordiga and the PCI executive were arrested in 1923. Having been elected as a parliamentary deputy for the Veneto, and therefore exempt from arrest, Gramsci returned to Italy in May 1925. On his arrival, he found that the majority of the Party still subscribed to Bordiga's 'purist' position. Over the following months Gramsci worked to establish a 'centrist' line within the Party which recognized that conditions in Italy were not the same as those in Russia and that revolutionary strategy should be tailored accordingly. This position would, as time went on, sit very uncomfortably with Stalin's insistence that international communism should be subordinated to the needs of Russia. He was also elected as the Party's general secretary.

Despite the Fascists' supremacy, a sharp increase in Communist Party membership during 1923 and 1924 suggested that a workers' revolution was still feasible. However, the majority of the opposition continued to believe that the Fascists were a traditional political party, and could be resisted by parliamentary means. This was revealed as a tragic illusion when Fascist assassins murdered the socialist deputy Matteotti for denouncing Mussolini's anti-democratic policies. As a consequence of this, opposition deputies left the parliament in the Aventine Secession, hoping to force the king into taking action against the Fascists. Gramsci, by contrast, argued that the seceded 'parliament' should call for a general strike which could lead to a concerted counter-attack against fascism. Yet the opposition could not agree, and Mussolini used the absence of genuine popular resistance to begin a fresh wave of repression, turning Italy into a single-party dictatorship within two years.

Around this time, Gramsci's private life changed again. Giulia had given birth to a son, Delio, and in 1925 Gramsci was able to travel to Moscow to see them for a short time. He returned to Rome to give his only parliamentary speech, in which he correctly noted that a law aimed at curtailing the Freemasons was actually a move to outlaw opposition parties. After the speech, Mussolini is reputed to have congratulated Gramsci on his speech. Gramsci is reputed to have ignored him (Fiori 1970: 196).

Giulia and Delio came to live in Rome, where Giulia's sister Tatiana was already resident. However, this short domestic interlude was rendered impossible by the continuing repression. Giulia was expecting a second child and returned to Moscow in late 1926. On 8 November, Mussolini drew up a list of deputies to be arrested. Despite his parliamentary immunity, Gramsci was placed in detention. His trial, in which he was accused of provoking class hatred and civil war, took place in Rome in 1928. For these offences, the prosecutor demanded that the law 'must prevent this brain from functioning for 20 years'. The trial was a foregone conclusion and Gramsci was sentenced to 20 years imprisonment. He was transferred to Turi in the south of the country and thence to Formia, halfway between Rome and Naples in 1933.

During his time in Turi, Gramsci found himself increasingly isolated from the Communist Party, now led by Togliatti, and withdrew from political discussion with his fellow political prisoners. It is likely that, had his true views been known (particularly his growing hostility to Stalin), he would have been expelled from the Party. Granted 'provisional freedom' on the grounds of ill health, Gramsci was moved to a supervised clinic in Rome in 1935 where he died of a stroke in 1937. He is buried in the Protestant Cemetery in Rome.

Gramsci's prison sentence was effectively a death penalty. More and more illnesses swarmed around his body, a situation made worse by the prison authorities' indifference. Compounding this agony, Gramsci's contact with his wife and children was irregular, not least because Giulia was susceptible to long bouts of mental illness and proved unwilling to return to Italy. He would never see his second son, Giuliano. A letter to Tatiana notes that being cut off from his family 'added a second prison to my life'. 'I was prepared for the blows of my adversaries', he writes, 'but not for the blows that would also be dealt me from completely unsuspected corners' (1979: 175). Yet despite this, Gramsci's brain did not cease functioning in 1928. It is a mark of the contingent, developing nature of Italian fascism that unlike millions of subsequent victims of totalitarianism, Gramsci was imprisoned, not murdered. With the help of the Cambridge economist Piero Sraffa, he was able to receive books and journals, and his sister-in-law Tatiana campaigned ceaselessly for his release and for improvements in his condition, eventually smuggling Gramsci's writings from his room at the clinic. These took the form of 33 notebooks, a total of nearly 3,000 pages of tiny, meticulous handwriting.

These *Prison Notebooks* are a fragmentary, incomplete record of Gramsci's mental efforts over a decade, written under the watchful eye of the prison censor, and reassembled years later by editors and translators. Yet despite the conditions of their production and publication, what makes the *Notebooks* among the most important and moving documents of the twentieth century is precisely their immediacy, their sense of *not* being disinterested but of transcending the confines of prison, of reaching beyond the failure of socialism and the triumph of fascism, to understand a contemporary situation and to remake it. Thus, the very different scraps of synthesis and analysis in the *Notebooks* – about intellectuals, language and linguistics, about literature and folklore, the Southern Question and the Risorgimento, about 'Americanism', 'Fordism' and most insistently hegemony – build towards a major understanding of power and meaning in the countries of advanced capitalism. Written in conditions of terrible personal and political defeat, the *Prison Notebooks* nevertheless validate Dante Germino's description of

Gramsci as 'someone who acknowledges himself to be weaker physically but not inferior intellectually and spiritually; his body may be imprisoned but not his mind . . . What makes man is the spirit of liberty and revolt' (Germino 1990: 128).

SUMMARY

This chapter has considered the social circumstances that shaped the development of Gramsci's thought. The relatively 'weak' form of democratic capitalism that emerged in Italy in the nineteenth century gave rise to particular authoritarian tendencies that were ultimately expressed through fascism, but which also allowed the development of an active working-class movement. Drawing lessons from the period of *trasformismo* and the failed uprisings of 1917 and 1920, Gramsci observed that radical change in a democracy needed specific, not general, forms of analysis and strategy. Engagement with the thought of Croce and Lenin gave form to this project. At the same time, the chapter has mapped out the ways in which Gramsci's life as an activist was bound up with these events, demonstrating that thought cannot be detached from political action.

2

CULTURE

This chapter asks why Gramsci turned to culture as a way of understanding how ruling groups win, maintain and sometimes lose their power. It reviews Karl Marx's work on the relationship between the economic 'base' and the cultural 'superstructure' and outlines Gramsci's more nuanced understanding of this relationship. The chapter moves on to discuss Gramsci's analysis of civil society and the distinction he draws between the 'war of position' and the 'war of manoeuvre'. Finally it considers the question of culture within a spatial framework, paying particular attention to Gramsci's views on the 'Southern Question' and the construction of a 'national-popular'.

BASE AND SUPERSTRUCTURE

To appreciate the originality of Gramsci's work, we need to consider its relationship to earlier Marxist thought. Although the previous chapter suggested that Croce was a major influence on the young Gramsci, we also know that he attended a course of lectures on Marx during his university years, and that Marxist ideas were widespread in the socialist circles in which he moved after 1914. While Marxism paid relatively little attention to culture during this period, it dealt extensively with two related categories, ideology and the superstructure.

It is important to understand that Marx's materialist understanding of forms of thought represents a break with previous idealist conceptions of consciousness. For the early Marx, idealist philosophy inverts the true order of things by arguing that only through our perceptions of the world does it become meaningful. In his work *The German Ideology* (co-authored with Friedrich Engels and first published in 1846) Marx turns this notion on its head by arguing that 'Life is not determined by consciousness, but consciousness by life' (Marx 1977: 164). By this he means that there are historic and social reasons for the appearance of particular ideas and forms of cultural practice, such as art and literature. It is no accident that Marx and Engels chose a theological metaphor to illustrate this argument ('the German philosophy descends from heaven to earth') since the German philosophers have not, for them, freed themselves from the religious illusion that ideas have an existence independent of social conditions. How, ask Marx and Engels, can people 'pass from the realm of God to the realm of man' (from illusion to a clear-sighted understanding of reality) if they cannot grasp that ideas have no autonomous existence? One reason that such a leap cannot be made, they contend, is that idealist philosophy is not disinterested. The German philosophers may maintain a pose of impartiality, but their ideas are really counterparts to the material domination exercised by people of their own class. 'The ideas of the ruling class', they write 'are in every epoch the ruling ideas . . . the class which has the means of material production at its disposal has control at the same time over the means of mental production' (ibid.: 176). Marx and Engels claim that the ruling ideas 'are nothing more than the ideal expression of the dominant material relationships, the dominant material relationships grasped as ideas' (ibid.). In other words, the ideas of bourgeois thinkers are simply reflections of bourgeois social life.

Over the following decade, Marx's thoughts on ideology built towards the argument that not only are modes of thought determined by economic relations, but various institutions have developed to disseminate these ideas and to maintain an unequal class society. Marx's argument turns on the existence of a level of primary economic activity, what he calls the 'base' or 'structure', which determines all legal, educational, artistic and political activities. To these he gives the name 'superstructure'. In his most famous account of the superstructure, found in the Preface to *A Contribution to the Critique of Political Economy* (first published in 1859), Marx argues that the sum total of economic relations 'constitutes the economic structure of society, the real foundation, on which rises a legal and political superstructure and to which correspond definite forms of social consciousness' (1977: 389).

Marx therefore argues that the economic base is the most powerful and crucial level of social life. It is the base that brings the superstructure into being and which gives it its character. In turn the superstructure works to maintain the existing economic structure and to disguise or legitimize the real conditions of economic exploitation. For example, slavery was the economic 'structure' of large parts of the Americas between the fifteenth and nineteenth centuries. This gave rise to laws about what a slave could and could not do, to academic theories about the nature of African and Native American people, to religious apologies for slavery and so on. For the most part these phenomena (the superstructure) reinforced the practice of slavery, while appearing to be autonomous of it.

To truly change society, the base would have to be fundamentally changed and this for Marx, writing in the context of industrial society, entailed workers seizing control of the 'means of production' (above all, the factories). It follows from this argument that superstructural changes – penal reform, say, or abolishing private education – could not in themselves be truly revolutionary. This is not to say that they would be unwelcome, but they would not change the essential characteristics of capitalist exploitation.

We may make a number of points about this base–superstructure relationship. First, as Marx expresses the idea, it seems too neatly corresponding, as if only cultural forms and practices originating in a particular economic moment can flourish. Yet older practices and forms of consciousness continue to circulate and exert force long after they have ceased to be directly functional to the economic structure, religion being a prominent example. Second, the superstructure is a vast area having, as Marx himself notes, 'infinite variations and gradations, owing to the effect of innumerable external circumstances, climatic and geographical influences, racial peculiarities etc.' (quoted in Strinati 1995: 135). These circumstances would seem to undercut the determining power of the base somewhat, since capitalist societies have developed in observably different, uneven ways. The base does not allow us therefore to predict the precise character of the superstructure.

Third, Marx's privileging of material production as the essential aspect of the economic base is dependent upon a particular image of factory labour and ignores the extent to which other forms of production have a major role in the 'base'. Aspects of modern society which seem to correspond to his notion of the superstructure, such as the leisure, communications, sport and entertainment industries, are themselves now major sectors within the economy. Finally, superstructural areas do not necessarily behave in a way that directly corresponds with the interests of capitalism. The law, schools and politics can certainly be imagined as sustaining capitalism by, for example, guaranteeing property rights, turning children into good workers and representing the interests of capitalism in parliament, but they can also prosecute environmental polluters, teach children to read and write, and legislate for a shorter working week. While it may be the case therefore that in origin these institutions served the purposes of capitalism, they now have a high level of independence and autonomy and have some influence over the economic base.

It is clearly the case, then, that a politically transformative project needs to pay serious attention to both the base and superstructure and not to assume that either level is decisive. Gramsci's already evolving ideas on this subject were given a sense of urgency by the failure of a number of workers' revolts and it is to this that we now turn.

WARS OF MANOEUVRE AND POSITION

The previous chapter noted that, among a number of uprisings between 1917 and 1921, only the Russian Revolution succeeded in forming a workers' state, and that in a country which had not reached the level of industrial development predicted by Marx as a prerequisite of socialist revolution. Elsewhere in the industrialized world, capitalist economies and parliamentary democracies retrenched themselves, at least until the rise of fascism. It was therefore clear to Gramsci that the revolutionary strategy adopted in Russia, which was in any case contingent upon the crisis provoked by the First World War, would not work in more mature democracies. In this approach, Gramsci differed from Bordiga's PCI faction, which continued to imagine that a workers' uprising would take place through a direct assault on the state, initiated and led by Communist insurgents. In a letter written in 1924, Gramsci argued that such a revolution could not happen because the western democracies had generated a complex array of political groups and institutions which would have to be disentangled from their relationship with bourgeois society before any revolution could succeed. In western Europe there were trade unions, social-democratic parties and a well-paid 'labour aristocracy'. The presence of these 'political super-structures' provided a brake on direct action and required the Italian revolutionary party to adopt a more long-term strategy than had been necessary for the Bolsheviks (Gramsci 1971: lxvi).

Gramsci therefore draws a distinction between the kind of revolutionary action that took place in Russia, and the kind needed in other countries. In Russia, the political superstructure was very poorly developed, 'primordial and gelatinous' as he puts it, and consequently there was little in the way of intermediaries between the Tsarist regime and its revolutionary opponents. The Bolsheviks did not have to win over these intermediaries and could therefore concentrate their efforts in taking control of the state. To this all-out frontal attack, Gramsci gives the name 'war of manoeuvre', but, mindful of how the Western Front had become bogged down in trench fighting during the First World War, he argues that such sudden trans-formations and lightning victories are rare. Instead, most revolutions have to proceed via a *war of position* fought out over a long period in the super-structure, in which meanings and values become the object of struggle. The western capitalist nations have predicted that there will be serious opposition to their rule and, he argues, organized themselves accordingly. Whereas in undeveloped societies there was an absence of intermediaries, modern capitalist regimes have developed a tightly woven network of practices and institutions which guard against internal disintegration and make revolution a political and psychological impossibility.

A number of points can be made about this distinction between the war of manoeuvre and the war of position. The first concerns the relationship between ideological struggle and armed revolution. Gramsci's usage of the distinction is somewhat contradictory. On the one hand, he argues that the war of position is needed to prepare the ground before an assault can be made on capitalist society (ibid.: 108), while on another occasion he argues that the war of position has decisively superseded frontal attack (ibid.: 239). While this second usage may make Gramsci's work useful to political movements that renounce revolutionary violence, it sits uncomfortably with the inescapable fact that Gramsci was a barricades militant. It also threatens to align the war of position with reformism, precisely the tendency that prompted Gramsci's break with the PSI. Ransome (1992) therefore makes the persuasive case that we should think of these two strategies as operating in combination with each other. At some moments, a long preparation is indeed needed to shape parts of the superstructure before a decisive action can be taken (when, for example, a political party carefully establishes positive relationships with the news media before an election). At other times, however, the frontal attack is only the precursor to a war of position.

The ultimate failure of Soviet communism lay in its inability to win the struggle for hegemony once it had overthrown the Tsarist regime, and its consequent resort to repression.

CIVIL SOCIETY

Until now, the discussion has concerned the political realm. But it is not just trade unions and moderate socialist parties that form the superstructure. The vast range of institutions that constitute what Gramsci calls 'civil society' are also superstructural. Civil society includes political organizations, but it also includes the church, the school system, sports teams, the media and the family. In some of his uses of the term, Gramsci argues that the state provides an important mechanism in connecting civil society to the economy, but at other times civil society becomes a more encompassing term than this. In Gramsci's widest definition of the term it is 'the ensemble of organisms commonly called "private"' (1971: 12) and it is therefore as much a matter of individual behaviour, tastes and values as it is a matter of regulated cultural institutions. Clearly this model of the superstructure is far removed from Marx's assertion that it is the set of institutions which transmit a monolithic bourgeois ideology. Civil society certainly includes the legal apparatus, but it also includes children's parties, shopping trips and going on holiday. As it becomes more and more a matter of 'everyday life', so it becomes increasingly difficult to recognize that civil society has some connection with the operations of power. The individual, writes Gramsci, must come to 'govern himself without his self-government thereby entering into conflict with political society – but rather becoming its normal continuation, its organic complement' (ibid.: 268).

Civil society thus overlaps significantly with Gramsci's category of common sense, which we shall examine in the next chapter. Gardening, for instance, is certainly bound up with issues of, among other things, home ownership, family life, nationality and consumerism, and therefore contains within it certain wisdoms about the world which are functional to modern capitalism. But it cannot be reduced to these things, and nor is it likely to be articulated in these terms. Rather than being expressed in terms of class, it may be expressed in terms of other social divisions such as gender or age, or in terms of other categories entirely, such as pleasure. Yet it is precisely in this private realm that ruling values seem most natural and therefore unchangeable. A corollary of this is that a transformative politics which could thoroughly penetrate this realm would be both successful and durable (you might ask yourself which social movements have achieved even a partial version of this transformation). 'Civil society' therefore implicitly acknowledges that there are issues in circulation other than that of class. Whereas for some earlier versions of the concept, civil society is only useful in sustaining an unequal society, Gramsci argues that a 'complex and well-articulated' civil society would be necessary even after a major upheaval.

THEORIST OF THE SUPERSTRUCTURES

This emphasis on civil society leads to a third point. For some writers, Gramsci inverts the base–superstructure relationship by arguing that civil society, rather than the economy, is the motor of history, for this is where the meanings and values that can sustain or transform society are created. Thus, for the Italian political philosopher Norberto Bobbio, 'the structure is no longer [in Gramsci] the subordinating moment of history, [instead] it becomes the subordinate one' (Bobbio 1979: 34). Moreover Bobbio argues that Gramsci awards much greater significance to ideas than to cultural institutions. In the process, Gramsci becomes closely aligned with the idealist tradition, since ideologies are no longer 'posthumous' justifications of a ruling class but instead 'forces capable of creating a new history and of collaborating in the formation of a new power' (ibid.: 36).

In some ways Bobbio's argument, which is an attempt to highlight Gramsci's originality, merges with the criticism, made typically by structuralist Marxists, that Gramsci pays insufficient attention to deep (or structural) forms of inequality and simply inverts the relationship between base and superstructure. However, we might suggest a number of caveats *vis-à-vis* the characterization of Gramsci as the 'theoretician of the superstructures'. First, as we shall see in a later chapter, Gramsci is a sufficiently orthodox Marxist to argue that crises within the economic structure generate new forms of organization and consciousness, though they do not determine their exact form. Moreover, far from rejecting Marx's Preface to the *Critique of Political Economy*, Gramsci treats it as foundational, repeatedly paraphrasing Marx's notion that capitalism is busy creating the economic conditions for its own overthrow ('Mankind only sets itself such tasks as it can solve'). It is the logic of capitalist development for both Marx and Gramsci that it generates 'political, religious, aesthetic or philosophical . . . forms in which men become conscious of conflict and fight it out' (Marx 1977: 389–90).

A second objection is that Bobbio seems to regard the economic base in a particularly limited way, with all forms of creativity occurring in the superstructure. Yet the world of labour and production cannot be abstracted from culture or creativity in quite so total a way. Production is organized 'culturally' (we can talk, for instance, about workplace cultures) and the design, purchase and use of commodities are themselves 'cultural' activities. Gramsci himself certainly did not conceive of production as an entirely machinic act of drudgery – how else could he have supported the Factory Councils? As Jacques Texier, the most prominent critic of Bobbio's work writes, people's creativity 'should not be understood merely on the "political" or superstructural level. It occurs . . . in the development of the productive forces of social work' (Texier 1979: 60).

Third, and most significant, Bobbio's idealist interpretation ignores those moments when Gramsci explicitly deals with base and superstructure as levels that interact as a circuit, rather than as linear determinants of each other. Gramsci develops the notion of the *historical bloc* to explain that base and superstructure have a 'dialectical' or 'reflexive' relationship. Base and superstructure constantly impact upon each other with no level assumed to be the primary level of determinacy. We have come some distance, then, from the idea that culture is overwhelmingly determined by the economic base (or, applying Gramsci's work, that cultures of race, age, gender and sexuality are entirely determined by the structured inequalities that define these differences). Without falling into the mistake of thinking that cultural practices are entirely autonomous of such structures, we can suggest that they have what the later Marxist thinker Louis Althusser (1918–90) would call 'relative autonomy' from the base. One relatively autonomous cultural area that had a particular resonance for Gramsci was the question of nation, which had become central to various political and aesthetic movements in his lifetime. I discuss this in the next section.

NATIONAL-POPULAR AND THE 'SOUTHERN QUESTION'

Whereas much Marxist thought is internationalist, Gramsci posed questions of culture and politics in national and regional terms. We have seen that he abandoned his early Sardism, while remaining conscious that the *Mezzogiorno* was systematically exploited by the North. This exploitation, he felt, was often represented as a question of taste, so that the South was held to have an inferior culture. To make Italy a genuinely progressive country, the poor

South needed to be integrated on its own terms, not just by the spread of northern industry and culture. For this reason, two further Gramscian terms, the Southern Question and the emergence of a national-popular will be treated as two inseparable aspects of the same problem. In our own time, the issue of globalization poses a very similar problem: a globalization that ignores national, regional and local difference is not one that will engage the hearts and minds of subaltern and subordinate people.

Gramsci's interest in the Southern Question was, in part, a consequence of his early interest in linguistics. During his degree course, he chose to study the Sardinian language under the 'neolinguist' Bartoli. As with Gramsci's political orientation, neolinguistics provided a counterpoint to the reigning positivism of the 'neogrammaticists'. For the neogrammaticists, phonic change was governed by exceptionless laws, and it was therefore logical for them that certain sorts of speech represented the highest development of the language. By contrast, the neolinguists were concerned with social factors in explaining how dominant speech communities, such as urban elites, exerted influence over regional dialects, and over the language of the urban and rural poor. As Franco Lo Piparo (1979) has argued, in their awareness that linguistic change occurred through the exercise of prestige rather than through coercion, the neolinguists strikingly prefigured Gramsci's understanding of hegemony. Yet what was notable about the development of the Italian language after Unification was precisely its failure to be actively accepted as a truly national language. Instead it continued to be the 'property' of the ruling class.

Not only did the majority of Italians see 'standard Italian' as belonging to an elite, but educational policy was revised in 1923 so that standard Italian grammar was no longer taught through the school system (while acknowledging its presence, Gramsci has little to say about how the mass media might play a complementary or alternative role in transmitting and reproducing the standard language). For Gramsci, this policy simply reinforced existing inequalities by ensuring that dialect-speaking children had no access to the national culture with its systems of academic and bureaucratic preferment. Moreover, for Gramsci, the horizons of someone who could speak only in a local language would always be constrained by their surroundings. A person, he writes, 'who only speaks dialect, or understands the standard language incompletely, necessarily has an intuition of the world which is more or less limited and provincial' (1971: 325). But equally, the person who could only speak the national language would be unable to communicate with dialect speakers and therefore unable to form any political bond with them. 'To form hegemony', writes Nadia Urbinati, means 'to enable communication among the cultural levels that make up a national culture. Hegemony aims at ensuring that no social group, whether intellectuals or southern peasants, remains a "narrow province"' (Urbinati 1998: 151).

Extending this argument, it is not just language itself which provides an obstacle, but the whole system of communication between different groups. For Gramsci, a failure to communicate between various groups had taken place not only in the Italian language but also in Italy's characteristic forms of literary and popular culture. He noted that Italy had not developed any of the genres of popular literature such as the romance, the thriller, science-fiction or children's literature. Although these genres were widely read in Italy, they tended to be translations from French or English. Gramsci explains this in a manner very similar to his thoughts on language, arguing that the cultural history of Italy was divided by class and regional lines. From the Middle Ages, a prestigious form of literary Italian developed, exemplified by Dante's *Divine Comedy* (c. 1306–21). This was, however, a culture of the elite, not of the people. He argues (and we might want to critically interrogate this assertion), that other European countries developed a more truly 'national-popular' literature. Shakespeare provides an example of national-popular cultural production, as do Tolstoy and Dostoevsky. For Gramsci, these writers and their audience or readership held the same conception of the world. This was not the case in Italy, where writers had no 'national-educative' function and did 'not set themselves the problem of elaborating popular feelings after having relived them and made them their own' (Gramsci 1985: 206–7).

However, there was one popular cultural form in which Italy excelled and which had a close family resemblance to the popular novel. This was the opera (particularly the popular operas of Giuseppe Verdi), and while Gramsci's notes sometimes betray a distaste for the medium, and for music more generally, he observes that opera successfully articulates the feelings of the people. Its 'baroque' manner, he writes, represents an 'extraordinarily fascinating way of feeling and acting, a means of escaping what they consider low, mean and contemptible in their lives and education in order to enter a more select sphere of great feelings and noble passions' (ibid.: 378). Because opera and popular song are non-literary cultural forms, they appealed to a population where, particularly in the South, illiteracy remained very high. Moreover, because it constructs a realm of 'feeling' rather than a realm of 'thought', opera bears a close resemblance to folklore, another area in which Gramsci felt that a national-popular needed to be constructed.

Gramsci's conception of folklore corresponds in many respects to the more expansive category of popular culture. He notes that while most intellectuals view folklore as 'picturesque' and old-fashioned, his own conception treats it as a living 'conception of the world and life' which stands in implicit opposition to 'official' conceptions of the world (ibid.: 189). Because subjugated people, and particularly semi-literate or illiterate people, lack the centralizing institutions (such as printing) which could standardize their conceptions of the world, folklore is unelaborated, deeply traditional, unsystematic and many-sided. Yet it is not dead or limited, for new scientific and social understandings will be incorporated into it, in however haphazard a fashion, and it is 'tenacious', providing people with a rich cultural and emotional orientation towards the world which is extremely difficult to change. Gramsci's purpose is not to simply endorse folklore, for he acknowledges that much of the culture of subordinate people is conservative and fatalistic. Instead he proposes that such 'fossilized' conceptions be disaggregated from those 'which are in the process of developing and which are in contradiction to or simply different from the morality of the governing strata' (ibid.: 190). Only by doing this could peasants and intellectuals be organized into part of the coalition in which communication could take place. Without it, Italy would remain a 'great social disintegration', in which the intellectuals regarded the peasants as bestial, cultureless 'machines to be bled dry', and the peasants, overwhelmed by fear, believed that learning was a trick unique to the intellectuals.

The construction of a national-popular therefore necessitated two linked operations: first to answer the Southern Question by synthesizing the cultures of North and South. This involved abandoning any assumptions about the superiority of Italian high culture, and the primitivism of the South. The second was to find currents within the culture of all the popular classes that had the potential to provide an alternative conception of the world. A cultural project, wrote Gramsci, could not be some avant-garde movement imposed upon people, instead it had to be rooted in the 'humus of popular culture as it is, with its tastes and tendencies and with its moral and intellectual world, even if it is backward and conventional' (ibid.: 102).

QUESTIONING THE 'NATIONAL-POPULAR'

Gramsci's notion of a national-popular culture has attracted a number of criticisms, and this section outlines the two most significant objections. The first is that Gramsci, and some thinkers who adopt a Gramscian line, are insufficiently critical of the concept of nationhood. There are indeed moments at which Gramsci seems to reproduce some questionable assumptions about nationhood, such as his claim that standard Italian is 'technically superior' to dialects and therefore forms the basis for a common language (1971: 39). More challenging is Paul Gilroy's (1987) criticism that some *uses* of the term 'national-popular' are insufficiently sensitive to the ways in which national identity is frequently saturated with racial connotations. Gilroy's analysis of Britain in the 1980s points out that the British Left's attempt to wrest an idea of Britishness away from the Conservative Party ignored the deeply sedimented connection within British culture between national identity, whiteness and racism.

Gilroy is clearly right to point out that national-popular projects are typically ethnically exclusive. And as the experience of imperialism shows, national-popular conceptions can be forcibly imposed on others. Moreover, as Gramsci could not predict, movements for national autonomy have proliferated in recent times. While these movements are sometimes peaceful and democratic, they are just as commonly committed to the violent pursuit of cultural and ethnic purity. Gramsci's socialist internationalism therefore seems to have little purchase on such developments, which point in the direction of a new 'great disintegration'.

However, this critique of actual practices of nation-building has a limited purchase on Gramsci's work itself, which is an attempt to explain and overcome the exclusions that are carried out in the name of nationhood. Whereas the Italian nation was formed in opposition to what was imagined as a cultureless South, Gramsci argues that no nation-building project will be successful if it does not integrate all the popular classes and groups into an active conception of their identity as people in place. It therefore acknowledges difference as an active component of the national-popular, and resists an idea of ethnic purity (unsurprisingly, given that Gramsci was himself a Sardinian of Albanian descent).

A second major criticism of 'national-popular' has been put forward by David Forgacs, who argues that Gramsci's work lacks a sense of mechanism. How, he asks, does one 'initially win the consent of other forces and movements [and] how can this will, once established, be . . . prevented from disintegrating back into competing sectoral interests?' (Forgacs 1993: 189). While Gramsci does not offer an explicit system for winning the consent of other groups, he does, as we have seen, suggest that without a sensitivity to the 'tastes and tendencies' within popular culture, national-popular projects will fail. So, for example, the close association of the British Labour government with the Millennium Dome in 1999–2000 was widely seen as a 'cosmopolitan' enthusiasm without roots in popular taste.

What Gramsci does not explain, beyond gestures to the future role of a centralizing political party, is how some 'molecular' events, which seem genuinely transformative, fail to produce lasting change. An example of such a temporary national-popular is provided by the football World Cup in 1998. France hosted the event against a backdrop of racial tension in the country, focused around support for the racist Front National (FN). Half the French squad were of foreign descent, including the talismanic Zinedine Zidane, who comes from the French-Algerian community. When the French pulled off a surprise victory against favourites Brazil, the result was represented as uniting the French into a 'rainbow nation' in which ethnic tensions between white, black and North African French people were overcome. While this certainly involved a degree of media and political opportunism (right-wing President Chirac, for example, saluted a 'tricolour and multicolour' team), it also contained genuinely popular currents – and provided a real rebuke to the FN which had agitated for a 'pure French' team. However, the positive feelings surrounding the event failed to translate into a new political conception of Frenchness. The goodwill generated by the victory dissipated and France has been caught up in further prominent ethnic tensions over the FN's second place in the 2002 presidential elections and the banning of the Islamic headscarf in state schools in 2004. There is, therefore, nothing guaranteed about 'nation-popular' projects: it has to be accepted that few blocs will become hegemonic for any length of time. We look at the instability of consent in the next chapter.

SUMMARY

In this chapter we have seen how Gramsci questions the notion that the economic base determines the operations of an ideological and cultural superstructure. He proposes instead that we see the relationship between base and superstructure as a reflexive and dynamic one. Within this formation, he isolates civil society as having a key intermediary role and proposes that both conservative and transformative projects attempt to occupy consciousness and everyday life through the functioning of a civil society created in their service. To change society involves a protracted period of negotiation carried out in all the institutions of society and culture. The chapter ended by focusing on the nation as a prominent focus for civil projects, arguing that Gramsci's understanding of the national-popular is always critical, since it involves elaborating subaltern and subordinate elements into a broader cultural and political project without dismissing their cultural distinctiveness.

3

HEGEMONY

This chapter analyses the central element of Gramsci's thought, his theory of hegemony. It maps the word's development from Russian and Italian sources to Gramsci's conception of it as cultural and political leadership. Gramsci's adoption of the term represents a break with the Marxist emphasis on ideology introduced in the previous chapter. Hegemony is a more sensitive and therefore useful critical term than 'domination', which fails to acknowledge the active role of subordinate people in the operation of power. The chapter proposes that Gramsci defines hegemony through a series of distinctions between different moments within the hegemonic process. It therefore isolates his notes on coercion and consent, domination and leadership, 'common sense' and 'good sense' and 'limited' and 'expansive' hegemony to show how these details build into a nuanced conception of political and cultural authority.

Since hegemony has been such a prominent and yet contested term within applications of Gramsci's work, the following two chapters will outline a series of case studies that show how a dynamic and reflexive understanding of cultural power, rooted in Gramsci's thought, has been put to use by thinkers in the humanities and social sciences. Although centred on theories of class, these case studies will discuss the usefulness of hegemonic theory to other forms of social division, particularly the analysis of gender and race. This chapter, however, is largely located within Gramsci's lifetime, demonstrating the genealogy of the term, issues relating to its meaning and the oppositions it seeks to reconcile.

THE ROOTS OF HEGEMONY

Previous chapters have demonstrated that Gramsci's thoughts on politics and culture were formed during a period of defeat: the crushing of workers' revolts in Europe, and the failure of the Italian working-class movement in its struggles with factory owners, with the Italian state and with Mussolini's Fascists. As we have seen, Gramsci's diagnosis of this defeat hinges on the inability of the working class to form alliances with other subordinate groups, particularly the peasantry and the intellectuals. Achieving such an alliance means overcoming the mutual misunderstandings and hostilities that separate these different groups. Gramsci argues that it is necessary to surmount these deep divisions in order to form a genuinely popular national organization which can defeat fascism and achieve a transformation of society. Crucially, however, this alliance is not simply a federation of factions that carry equal weight. The industrial working class *lead* their allies (or, more precisely, their *subalterns*) through ideological means and provide the centre of any progressive movement. This, in its simplest form, is what he means by 'hegemony'.

Gramsci was not the originator of the concept of hegemony. The term had a long history in the Russian socialist movement and was given fresh theorization by Lenin (see box). Gramsci almost certainly encountered debates about the term during his period in Moscow.

LENIN

Vladimir Ilyich Ulyanov or 'Lenin' (1870–1924) was the founder of the Bolshevik tendency within the Russian Social Democratic Labour Party, a faction which evolved into the Russian Communist Party. Returning from exile in 1917, Lenin was – with Trotsky (1879–1940) – the major figure of the October Revolution that overthrew the provisional government, established in the wake of Tsar Nicholas II's abdication. Lenin prosecuted the Civil War of 1918–20 and supervised the reconstruction policies that followed it. Operating as a virtual dictator, he silenced opposition parties and hostility from within the Communist Party, laying the foundations for the more systematic repression of the Stalin years. As a theorist, his legacy has continued to be significant, covering such issues as the development of a disciplined revolutionary party and the meanings

Lenin, in fact, rarely uses the term 'hegemony' explicitly, though Gramsci claimed that 'Ilich' (the name he used for Lenin in the *Prison Notebooks*), was responsible for 'the concept and the fact of hegemony' (1971: 381). By this, Gramsci meant three things. First, that Lenin understood that revolution would not happen simply as a reflex of developing 'contradictions' within the economy (the positivist misconception known as 'economism'). Instead, he gave due consideration 'to the front of cultural struggle'. Second, Lenin developed the idea that the bourgeoisie was as committed to the struggle for hegemony as its opponents, attempting to lead the working class through its control of ideas and institutions. Lenin writes that 'the working class spontaneously gravitates towards socialism; nevertheless, bourgeois ideology, which is the most widespread (and continuously revived in the most diverse forms), is the one which, most of all spontaneously imposes itself upon the working class' (cited in Holst 1999: 414) – this despite the fact that Russia lacked the western democracies' developed civil societies, through which such notions could be disseminated and embedded.

Third, Lenin argued that the revolutionary party must adopt the struggles of *all* oppressed groups and classes, not just the economic struggle of the industrial working class. He maintained that it is only possible to understand the oppression of the working class through understanding the 'relationships between all the classes and strata and the state and the government, the sphere of the interrelations between all the classes' (ibid.: 416). In the case of Russia in 1917, this meant linking the discontents of the industrial working class with the desires of the peasantry for land redistribution, of the soldiers for peace and of the oppressed nationalities, such as the Ukrainians, Finns and Latvians, for freedom from Russian rule.

Gramsci was certainly a 'Leninist' to some extent. In particular he saw the political party as having a major role in educating allied groups and thereby cementing its leadership of the working class. In certain conditions, he writes, parties arbitrate between the interests of their own group and of other groups, thereby 'securing the development of the group which they represent with the consent and assistance of the allied groups' (1971: 148).

Gramsci did not, however, simply parrot those ideas of hegemony developed by Lenin. Richard Bellamy (1994) points out that the word had currency within nineteenth-century Italian thought, particularly in the writings of the Moderate Catholic philosopher Vincenzo Gioberti, who used it to suggest that one region within a nation could exert 'moral primacy' over others. Not only was this a justification for the unification of Italy under Piedmontese leadership, but it also linked the idea of hegemony with the development of a national-popular culture. Thus, for Gramsci, 'Gioberti, albeit vaguely, has the concept of the Jacobin (see box) 'national-popular', of political hegemony, namely the alliance between bourgeoisie-intellectuals and the people' (1985: 248). Gioberti's work represented a search within Italian history for moments of hegemony. Likewise, Gramsci's work, while on the one hand a political tool for the construction of a revolutionary popular coalition, is also a tool of historical and cultural analysis, enabling us to evaluate those strategies by which different groups attempted to form hegemonic blocs in the past.

JACOBINISM

The Jacobins were the radical bourgeois faction during the French Revolution. Led most notably by Maximilien Robespierre (1758–94), they are most famous for instituting the 'Reign of Terror' during their domination of the National Assembly. Gramsci regularly uses the terms Jacobin and Jacobinism, but not always consistently. In his pre-prison writings, Jacobinism tends to be equated with abstraction and elitism amongst some left-wing groups. In the *Prison Notebooks*, however, Jacobinism becomes synonymous with an expansive hegemony of the popular classes under party leadership. He writes that not only did the Jacobins 'make the bourgeoisie the dominant class . . . [but] they [also] created the bourgeois state, made the bourgeoisie into the leading, hegemonic class of the nation, in other words gave the new state a permanent basis and created the compact modern French nation' (1971: 79). It is arguable that this estimation downplays the Jacobins' use of coercion to establish a centralized administration and army.

Gramsci's understanding of hegemony was, therefore, influenced by both native and international uses of the word. But he also added his own unique understanding of the term, blending other thinkers' understanding of the term with the intellectual currents discussed in the previous chapter: the need for a war of position, the role of civil society and the Southern Question.

HEGEMONY: OVERVIEW

This section describes and evaluates Gramsci's use of hegemony as a tool for historical and political analysis. Although, as we shall see, Gramsci's use of the term changes both over time and in relation to his subject matter, the last piece of writing before his arrest, 'Some Aspects of the Southern Question', is unambiguous about the nature of hegemony. The working class, he writes can only 'become the leading and the dominant [i.e. hegemonic] class to the extent that it succeeds in creating a system of class alliances which allows it to mobilize the majority of the working population against capitalism and the bourgeois State' (Gramsci 1994: 320). Because of the historical development of Italian society, this was not a struggle that could be purely posed in terms of economic inequality. In order to lead other groups within the working population, in particular the Italian peasantry, the working-class movement had to understand those issues that were culturally important to the peasants, and make them their own. The two issues that he identifies are the Southern Question and the role of the Catholic Church. It was within these matters that the peasantry experienced their oppression most forcefully, and the industrial proletariat therefore had to incorporate hostility to these inequalities into its programme and place the demands of the peasantry among its objectives.

Far from dominating its junior partners, therefore, a successful hegemonic group has to thoroughly recreate itself. It is not a question of cynically speaking on behalf of other groups' desires in order to capture their vote, or of selecting certain issues in order to appeal to a broader constituency; a truly hegemonic group or class really must make large parts of its subalterns' worldview its own. In the course of this, the leading group will itself become changed, since its narrow factionalism (what Gramsci calls 'corporatism') has been translated into a much broader, even universal, appeal. To achieve leadership, workers have to stop thinking of themselves as, say, metalworkers or carpenters, or even just as workers. Instead

> They must think as workers who are members of a class which aims to lead the peasants and intellectuals. Of a class which can win and build socialism only if it is aided and followed by the great majority of these social strata.
>
> (Gramsci 1994: 322)

This very broad definition of leadership throws up a number of issues. First, it grants a leading group the power to make choices and act collectively, a capacity known as *agency*. People in leading groups are granted a good degree of clarity in seeing a situation as it is, rather than being impaired by structural constraints or by the operations of ideology. Second, to genuinely engage with the culture of subaltern groups means treating seriously those practices and values that are meaningful to them, but which are by no means necessarily progressive. As we have seen, Gramsci identifies the Catholic Church as a major institution and set of ideas that exert force over the everyday lives of the peasantry. Yet, despite his own atheism, Gramsci did not see the Church as automatically reactionary. Early in his Socialist career, Gramsci rejected a mindless anti-clericalism and fostered links with Church activists, recognizing that most Italians were believers. Similarly, 'Aspects of the Southern Question' makes the point that the Church in Italy was itself divided along regional lines. In the South, priests often acted as a layer of feudal oppression, since they were themselves middle-class landlords. In the North, however, the Church often fulfilled a different role, providing a form of democratic and ethical-spiritual opposition to the state.

You might ask yourself whether any political formations today hold together uneasy bedfellows, and analyse the strategies that are deployed to maintain such alliances. An example from Britain would be the anti-war coalition that formed around the 2003 invasion of Iraq, and which temporarily united secular leftists with many Muslims. The perception that Islamic membership of the alliance compromised the Left's commitment to gay and women's rights was hotly contested by the coalition's organizers, who argued that Muslim social conservatism should not prevent collaboration over hostility to the war.

Third, we might ask to what extent are subalterns incorporated into the worldview of a dominant group? What if a ruling group is forced to grant too many economic or ideological concessions to those it leads? What if a subaltern group develops the necessary agency to lead a hegemonic struggle itself and to challenge the authority of a 'fundamental' group such as the proletariat or the bourgeoisie (Gramsci observes that 'some part of a subaltern mass is always directive and responsible')? If this were to happen, then over the long war of position, the leading group will be transformed out of all recognition. Socialist politics today, for example, typically involves a broad coalition of the Left involving, among others, feminists, gay rights campaigners, peace activists, representatives of ethnic minorities and environmentalists. But maintaining the primacy of class among these various interests is far from straightforward – socialism begins to look like just one alternative position among many, or comes to be defined precisely as a rainbow alliance of equal interests.

Moreover, political groups and parties do not simply face downwards towards the oppressed. In their electoral appeals to businesses and middle-class voters, the American Democrats and British Labour Party have been accused of taking on board the perspectives of those they sought to hegemonize. Thus, these parties, and others like them, experience transformism as they switch from being a hegemonic bloc to being a bloc hegemonized by multinational capitalism and middle-class conservatism. We may also observe that the attempt by one region to lead another sometimes has unanticipated counter-hegemonic consequences. Subaltern regions (or more precisely the elites of subaltern regions) exert hegemonic pressures of their own in, for example, the devolved governments of the UK, the American South, the Spanish *autonomías* (regional governments), and, indeed, in the Italian *Mezzogiorno*.

In fact Gramsci has no conclusive answer to how 'fundamental' groups can limit the hegemonic activities of those it seeks to lead and restrict the 'expansiveness' of its hegemony. The inability to fully theorize this problem is suggested by one of Gramsci's rare resorts to economism. Noting that 'account [must] be taken of the interests of the groups over which hegemony is to be exercised', and that 'the leading group should make sacrifices of an economic-corporate kind', Gramsci still concludes that 'such sacrifices and such a compromise cannot touch the essential', which is 'the function exercised by the leading group in the decisive nucleus of economic activity' (1971: 161).

Despite this atypical reductiveness, it is precisely the porosity of a hegemonic bloc to the demands of others which provides a cause for optimism. A ruling power that asks for consent and yet which cannot give voice to the aspirations of those in whose name it rules will not survive indefinitely. Gramsci's argument that, within the hegemonic process, subalterns pass from being 'a thing' to being 'a historical person, a protagonist' is a powerful counter to the mass culture position that subalterns are ideologically dominated by their leaders. It is a sign of Gramsci's democratic impulse that he argues that a hegemonizing group must accept challenges to its leadership. 'Active and direct consent', he writes, means 'the participation of all, even if it produces a disintegration or an apparent tumult' (in Buci-Glucksmann 1982: 119).

The issue of subaltern people's aspirations points us to a fourth point about hegemony: it is a process without an end. In order to maintain its power, a leading group must be constantly alert to the volatile demands of its subalterns and to the shifting context within which it exerts its authority. A social group, Gramsci writes, has to exercise leadership before it wins power, but even when it has won power 'it must continue to "lead" as well' (1971: 58).

A fifth question would be broadly psychological. Why, we might ask, do people accept the leadership of others? Why do they substantially adopt the hegemonic bloc's worldview as their own? One answer to this is that hegemony is not simply a question of meanings and values: it also takes economic, material and legal-political forms. A ruling power that ensures that its subordinates have enough to eat, are in paid employment and have adequate access to healthcare, childcare and holidays has gone a long way towards winning their hearts and minds. Equally, parliamentary democracies appear to grant subordinate people a good degree of legal-political autonomy through granting them various rights and through allowing them to vote, to regularly change their government and to stand for election themselves. 'What uniquely distinguishes the political form of such societies', observes Terry Eagleton, 'is that people are supposed to believe they govern themselves' (Eagleton 1991: 112). It is arguable that other forms of society also foster such an illusion, but Eagleton perceptively directs our attention to the institutional dimension of hegemony.

For within the 'ideological' operation of hegemony, organizations also contribute to the dissemination of meanings and values. We saw in the previous chapter that Gramsci identified civil society as a key mechanism for the maintenance of authority, and suggested that its effectiveness lies in the way it blurs the distinction between political authority and everyday life. What takes place in our homes, in our leisure activities or in the shops seems, for the most part, apolitical. There is no need for someone to experience a blinding conversion to an idea – it is often already deeply enmeshed in the structure of their lived reality. What strikingly distinguishes Gramsci from some of his near-contemporaries is his refusal to take these forms of semi-conscious, collective behaviour as evidence that people are the dupes of ruling powers. While for Gramsci's German Marxist contemporaries Theodor Adorno (1903–69) and Max Horkheimer (1895–1973), mass culture is evidence both of capitalism's power and of people's unthinking conformity, Gramsci makes the anti-elitist case for everyone being part of a mass: 'We are all conformists', he writes, 'of some conformism or other, always man-in-the-mass or collective man' (1971: 324).

The task for Gramsci is to understand the positive and negative currents and modes of thought caught up within each historical type of conformism. Take, for example, the role of the car in everyday life. The automotive industry is a key sector of the capitalist economy and most people would probably agree that high levels of car ownership have negative consequences for the environment and for more vulnerable road users. Nonetheless, people in the developed world continue to use cars in large numbers and resist using other forms of transport. This is not entirely a consequence of the false ideas imposed upon people by the manufacturers of cars, nor evidence of overwhelming selfishness. It is also the case that the car is the technology that puts people most directly in contact with the scattered institutions of civil society – with supermarkets, extended families, schools, clinics and the dispersed social networks that make up the landscape of our world. It is the apparently *freely chosen* nature of this mobility, and the way that it is bound up with human relationships of love and care that makes its ties so binding.

A final point to raise about Gramsci's conception of hegemony concerns the question of force. What is a hegemonic group to do with those groups that cannot be assimilated into its cultural and political project? He writes that while a hegemonic bloc *leads* coalition groups, it '*dominates* antagonistic groups, which it tends to "liquidate", or to subjugate perhaps even by armed force' (1971: 57). What, therefore, is the distribution of coercion and consent within his theory of hegemony? The next section explains why Gramsci felt that, within modern societies, the emphasis has shifted decisively to the latter term.

COERCION AND CONSENT

In the *Prison Notebooks*, Gramsci makes an oblique comparison between Communist Party strategy and a work of Renaissance political theory, Machiavelli's *The Prince* (see box). He argues that the Party must become a 'Modern Prince' in uniting the popular currents within Italian national life.

MACHIAVELLI

Although the work of the diplomat and statesman Niccolò Machiavelli (1469–1527) has become synonymous with political scheming, he was a central point of reference for both Gramsci and Mussolini. Machiavelli's major work, *The Prince*, was written in 1513 as an attempt to curry favour with Florence's ruling Medici family. It proposes that monarchs should retain absolute control of their territory and use any means to achieve this goal. Gramsci saw Machiavelli's life and work as having a number of parallels with his own. Written within a period of foreign invasion and internal disunity, *The Prince* ends with an impassioned demand for Italian unity. Machiavelli's *Discourses on Livy* (1517) make the case for a politically active citizenry inspired by national idealism and his *Art of War* (1520) advocates the formation of a citizen soldiery which would replace foreign mercenaries. For Gramsci, Machiavelli was a 'precocious Jacobin', an 'integral politician' and 'revolutionary' who, by understanding the need to bring the peasantry into national life, helped to make the Renaissance into a mass cultural movement.

In one passage, Machiavelli discusses how a successful ruler must combine an appeal to people's values with control over the means of violence. He adopts the mythological figure of the Centaur – half man and half horse – to illustrate this. A ruler, he writes, 'must know well how to imitate beasts as well as employing properly human means' (Machiavelli 1988: 61).

At the point in the *Prison Notebooks* at which he discusses this 'dual perspective', Gramsci concedes that leadership involves combining the level of force with that of consent. He dismisses the idea that these two levels correspond to different periods in the exercise of a group's power (though elsewhere he proposes the existence of a 'moment of force' at which the mode of control shifts decisively towards brutality). Gramsci's use of Machiavelli therefore argues for the indivisibility of coercion and consent. If consent is organized through civil society, then coercion is the responsibility of what Gramsci calls *political society*. He defines political society as the set of apparatuses which legally enforce discipline on those groups who do not give their consent during a normative period, and which dominate the whole of society in periods when consent has broken down. This suggests that the cultural, economic and political aspects of hegemony are, in the last instance, always underpinned by the threat of violence. While this analysis undoubtedly holds true for certain sorts of politics and in certain situations (for example, in violent confrontations between the police and demonstrators, or the eruption of violence between different ethnic groups), it is open to question whether a dualism of coercion and consent is a valuable way of thinking about *all* hegemonic processes. The lack of consistency within Gramsci's usage of this distinction suggests that he found the coercion/ consent couplet troubling, and we might suggest two reasons why this is the case.

First, the opposition between coercion and consent can be dismantled. For the most part, coercive apparatuses in modern societies, such as the police, courts and armed forces, operate with a high level of consent. In the UK, for example, it is common for people to demand more, not less police officers, and in part this is a product of the circulation of benign images of the police within civil society. Similarly, when the British newspaper the *Daily Mirror* ran a story in 2004 purporting to show British troops abusing Iraqi prisoners of war, the resulting popular outrage led to the dismissal of the newspaper's editor. In part this was because the army exerts its own consensual authority within British national life. In language that strikingly echoes Gramsci's conception of hegemony as moral and intellectual leadership, the centre-left *Observer* noted that the British officer corps 'insist[s] that the job of leaders is unambiguously to establish objectives, achieve common intent through moral relationships of integrity and then delegate' (Hutton 2004: 36). Indeed, at times Gramsci acknowledges that this coercion and consent are porous to each other. We have seen already that the peaceful struggle for hegemony is presented as a 'war of position', and Gramsci likens civil society to a trench system. Equally, he notes that subaltern groups and individuals must actively give their consent to the use of force, and express their consent through cultural values. Thus, 'the more an individual is compelled to defend his own immediate physical existence, the more he will uphold and identify with the highest values of civilization and humanity, in all their complexity' (1971: 170).

A second objection to seeing hegemony as being composed of both coercion and consent is that the balance between the two in modern democracies seems to have shifted markedly away from the overt use of force. Governments cannot coerce their opponents without risking a severe loss of ideological credibility. You might ask yourself, for example, whether government attempts to stifle news coverage of potentially uncomfortable stories are effective – or whether they rebound embarrassingly, and call into question the leadership of the politicians and bureaucrats. A successful hegemonic formation will be one in which conflict is minimized, since hegemony is dependent upon the existence of an 'individual who can govern himself without his self-government entering into conflict with political society' (1971: 268). Gramsci's more common definition of hegemony is consequently of a situation synonymous with consent. Civil society, he argues, corresponds to the function of hegemony, while political society corresponds to 'domination'.

Yet while Gramsci here relegates coercion to the 'moment of force', we might wish to retain a softer version of his notion of hegemony as a Centaur. We have already seen that the coercive apparatuses have a consensual role to play within civil society. Moreover, ruling powers and their opponents do make regular use of coercion, although rarely in Gramsci's sense of armed or judicial force. Instead, hegemony frequently relies on what the French sociologist Pierre Bourdieu (1930–2002) called 'symbolic violence'. This might take a number of forms. As we shall see in Key Idea 5, texts perform symbolic violence in the exclusions they perform and the silences they impose upon outsider groups. But symbolic violence also takes the form of taste judgements, where outsiders are marginalized and shamed; of physical behaviour and 'ways of living' where some feel confident and others feel awkward; and in the unequal distribution of educational qualifications. In these cases, a ruling power (particularly, for Bourdieu a ruling class) will see its authority reproduced, a subaltern group will aspire to the values and tastes of its superiors, and a 'dominated' group will see its lowly status reinforced.

LIMITED AND EXPANSIVE HEGEMONY

If a ruling group has to resort to coercion and repression, then it has not achieved an 'expansive' hegemony in which great masses of people spontaneously and actively give their consent to the bloc. To understand the opposite of this – limited hegemony – we need to return to Italy in the nineteenth century. During this period, writes Gramsci, the Moderate Party secured its hegemony over the other forces that had fought for unification, particularly the radical Action Party. What this involved was the practice of *trasformismo*, discussed in Key Idea 1. The formation of an expanded ruling group centred on the Moderates' political programme involved the gradual absorption of the leadership of allied and even antagonistic groups. This form of hegemony was limited, since the hegemonic class failed to genuinely adopt the interests of the popular classes and simply neutralized or 'decapitated' them through depriving them of their leadership. Roger Simon (1982: 53–4) has offered a similar analysis of the working-class movement in Britain, noting that right-wing leaders of the trade unions and the Labour Party have regularly won workers' support for the maintenance of capitalism through the offer of social reforms.

We can extend the notion of limited hegemony beyond the boundaries of class politics. A government may make some environmental reforms without fundamentally altering its environmental policy, or give token political representation to women or ethnic minorities. These strategies too seek to neutralize or decapitate the demands of subaltern groups.

The alternative to this is an 'expansive' hegemony in which a hegemonic group adopts the interests of its subalterns in full, and those subalterns come to 'live' the worldview of the hegemonic class as their own. In this situation, 'a multiplicity of dispersed wills, with heterogeneous aims, are welded together with a single aim, on the basis of an equal and common conception of the world' (quoted in Mercer 1984: 9). We have already noted that such formations are potentially unstable, as subaltern groups seek to challenge the authority of 'fundamental' groups. But it should be clear that only by expanding a programme can it become fully embedded in people's lives.

Tony Bennett (1986a) has given an example of such a moment of expansive hegemony in his analysis of holiday-making in Blackpool. He argues that the factory owners of the nineteenth century established a northern regional hegemony in England, in opposition to the aristocratic culture that characterized the south of England. Working people were 'condensed' into this regional hegemony through annual outings and holidays, during which the whole working population of northern industrial towns would travel *en masse* to Blackpool. There they encountered an image of the North as fundamentally modern; an image built into the town's architecture and its pleasures. Although these activities effectively tied people into the world of work, and therefore reproduced and reinforced the power of capitalism, holidays were not experienced in this way. Instead they were understood and desired as intrinsically Northern expressions of enterprise, endeavour and cheerfulness. The fact that this identity could be combined with a seemingly contradictory identity as members of the British Empire did not lessen its force. As we shall see now, Gramsci was perfectly aware of the contradictions of thought.

COMMON SENSE AND GOOD SENSE

The previous chapter discussed Gramsci's contention that folklore is a key form in which people's worldviews are stored and transmitted. As a living 'conception of the world and life', folklore overlaps significantly with his category of common sense. Common sense is indeed, he writes, 'the "folklore" of philosophy', since, like philosophy, it is a way of thinking about the world that is grounded in material realities. Unlike philosophy, however, common sense is unsystematic, heterogeneous, spontaneous, incoherent and inconsequential, a 'chaotic aggregate of disparate conceptions' that holds together 'Stone Age elements', the principles of advanced science and 'intuitions of a future philosophy' (1971: 324). We should not confuse Gramsci's notion of common sense with its normal use in English. Gramsci emphatically does not conceive of common sense as practical wisdom that contradicts theorizing or dogma. Instead it is literally thought that is common – common to a social group, or common to society as a whole. Thus, although he is largely interested in the common sense of the popular classes, and how a hegemonic bloc can intervene in it and shape it to their ends, he acknowledges that every social stratum has its common sense which is 'continually transforming itself, enriching itself with scientific ideas and with philosophical opinions which have entered ordinary life' (ibid.: 326).

As well as being internally contradictory, a person or group may have more than one common sense. Gramsci notes that a working person may have two theoretical consciousnesses: one implicit within the labour that is performed and another that has been inherited from the past and which influences their moral conduct. The institutions of civil society must therefore try to reshape themselves in order to accommodate the uneven and multiple forms of common sense. For Gramsci it is again the Catholic Church that works hardest to hold together what is in fact a 'multiplicity of distinct and often contradictory religions'. Similarly, in many societies today, it is the popular media that attempts such an integration of the diverse strands of common sense. It has been widely noted, for example, that the British tabloid press manifests a contradictory but consistent line on sexual attitudes, in which a notion of sex as harmless fun is accompanied both by a moralizing interest in celebrity infidelity and by demands for the most severe penalties for sex offenders. For Gramscian analysis, such condensed expressions of common sense are a cynical exercise in leadership, since they simply mimic the unevenness of popular consciousness with the intention of shaping its 'crudely neophobe and conservative' attitudes in a politically conservative direction. A more expansively hegemonic project would attempt to disarticulate the reactionary elements of common sense from the positive strands within it. To these progressive innovations he gives the name good sense.

Good sense, in fact, is much nearer to the standard English meaning of common sense. How, Gramsci asks, could people survive if their ideas and concepts about society were all false? It is logical that there must be a kernel of practical understanding in most people's conception of the world. Simply in order to be ruled, a person must actively participate in a particular conception of the world. A transformative project (what, in his coded near-synonym for Marxism, he calls a 'philosophy of praxis') must take hold of these ways of being in the world since they have a responsible, thoughtful element to them. This is vital not only to those who are being hegemonized, but also to the hegemonic bloc itself. One danger with a progressive project is that it may appear intellectualized and abstract rather than concrete and grounded. To guard against this tendency, an engagement with, and elaboration of, what he calls the 'simple' must take place, for the simplicity of good sense is connected to its role within practical life. Furthermore, good sense has an affective or emotional aspect which is absent from abstract theorizing. The intellectual must combine the *feelings* that are prominent within good sense (including the good sense of popular cultural representations) with his or her philosophical understanding of a situation. Gramsci argues that any educational project that is not rooted in concrete experience and popular conceptions is 'like the contacts of English merchants and the negroes of Africa' since a fair exchange does not take place. The only way, he argues, in which the gap between leaders and lead can properly be bridged is if the intellectuals are themselves *organic* to those they educate and persuade. We shall look in more detail at this aspect of Gramsci's thought in Key Idea 6.

SUMMARY

This chapter has made clear the distinction between domination and hegemony. It has argued that hegemony is moral and intellectual leadership which treats the aspirations and views of subaltern people as an active element within the political and cultural programme of the hegemonizing bloc. This understanding of hegemony as an ongoing form of negotiation represents an advance on conceptions of power which see it as the static possession of a particular social group. The chapter has shown that Gramsci used a series of oppositions (limited/expansive, coercion/consent, common sense/good sense) to highlight the nuances within the term. It has suggested issues within Gramsci's conception of hegemony around the maintenance of the fundamental group's authority and around the mechanisms by which subalterns accept the leadership of another group. The following chapter puts these questions into motion.

4

HEGEMONY IN PRACTICE 1: IDENTITY

The next two chapters review a series of case studies, looking at how hegemony has been applied to particular cultural forms and practices. Not all of these studies make overt use of Gramsci's work, and in some cases their theoretical frameworks are provided by the work of other thinkers. In all cases, however, their understandings of cultural power are sufficiently aligned with Gramsci's ideas to make them meaningfully 'Gramscian' or 'neo-Gramscian'. Equally, those studies that make their indebtedness to Gramsci explicit are not always pure reproductions of his work. Instead they are likely to treat his conception of hegemony flexibly and critically. This may be through combining Gramsci's work with that of other theorists, through deploying hegemonic theory to illuminate new cultural practices and forms, or through accentuating elements within Gramsci's analysis which may conflict with other features of his work, or with its overall direction.

Most pertinently, while Gramsci's theory of hegemony is primarily concerned with questions of class and nationhood, this chapter will also look at the application of his work to studies of youth, gender, 'race' and ethnicity. This should not be thought of as representing a dilution of hegemonic theory. As the British cultural theorist Stuart Hall has suggested, the Gramscian tradition's strength lies less in concrete and invariable propositions than in a willingness to revise and renovate theoretical frameworks of all kinds. '[Gramsci's] work', he argues, 'is of a "sophisticating kind" . . . it has a direct bearing on the question of the "adequacy" of existing social theories, since it is precisely in the direction of "complexifying existing theories and problems" that his most important theoretical contribution is to be found' (Hall 1996: 411). To use Gramsci's work outside its temporal and spatial contexts involves just such a 'complexifying' readjustment.

The narrative of the two chapters moves from a discussion of how individuals and groups are positioned by particular hegemonic practices to consideration of the roles of texts and cultural institutions in this process. This chapter considers how people establish identities within and against a hierarchically ordered society. The following chapter makes more explicit the role of representation in this process, and also how texts act out their own versions of leadership and consent, symbolically resolving real social conflicts through their narratives, sounds and images. It concludes by discussing the regulatory role played by the institutions of civil and political society, demonstrating how different interest groups – even groups *within* a leading bloc – compete with one another for authority. In all cases, you should be aware that these topics are being isolated for the purposes of explanation: in practice they cannot be so easily distinguished. People's identities, for example, are always produced, at least in part, through representation and through their multiple relationships with the institutions of the state and civil society: there is no 'pure' moment of identity that stands outside these other processes (see du Gay *et al*.'s [1997] discussion of the 'cultural circuit' for a more comprehensive account of this interdependence). Nonetheless, questions of identity have a particularly privileged position within both hegemonic activities and theories of hegemony. It is therefore to identity that I turn first.

BEING 'EXCELLENT'

While the following section considers the characteristics of resistance, here we analyse the production of 'subaltern' identities. These are the identities of those groups and individuals whose active consent is needed for the maintenance of a leading group's authority, and who therefore form a part – albeit a subordinate part – of the power bloc. If a hegemonic project is truly expansive, then this group will feel a strong bond of identification with the meanings and values of the leading group within the bloc (what is some-times called the 'hegemon'). The section lacks the space to consider the full range of forms and strategies through which this appeal to heterogeneous subaltern groups might operate. Instead it will isolate one prominent motif within attempts to win over a particularly valued subaltern group, the contemporary middle class. A set of discourses and practices, initially emerging in the world of work, and gradually spreading into other areas of social and cultural life, has explicitly sought to bind this class of workers and consumers to a moral, political and economic project that coheres around the terms 'enterprise' and 'excellence'. This section therefore evaluates the role of hegemony in people's acceptance, rejection and negotiation of enterprise culture.

As Paul du Gay (1991) has observed, the context for the emergence of 'excellence' was a downturn in the economic performance of a number of western countries in the 1970s. Demonstrating the Gramscian insistence that the economy cannot be wholly determinant, this economic crisis was indissolubly linked with a perceived cultural crisis, in which established values were called into question. Although individual national narratives differed, there was some consensus in the western democracies that the development of welfare institutions after the Second World War, the existence of inflexible practices amongst both management and trade unions, and the 'permissive society' of the 1960s had become serious obstacles to reversing economic and cultural decline. As Graeme Salaman (1997) notes, this feeling of decline was compounded in the USA by common assumptions about America's leading competitor, Japan. Japanese workers, it was argued, identified strongly with an ethic of hard work and with the values of their employer corporations.

The prescription for reversing these various declines was therefore twofold: first, to roll back some of the welfare developments of the previous half-century and, second, to promote a culture of excellence with which people and institutions would strongly identify. Du Gay, for example, notes that economic and moral regeneration 'necessitated exerting pressure on every institution to make it supportive of Enterprise' (1991: 45). If you are reading this book as part of a programme of further or higher education, you might interrupt your reading in order to look at your institution's prospectus, mission statement or annual report. Having done so, judge for yourself the extent to which the language of enterprise and excellence has penetrated its public pronouncements. You will find such discursive commitment to excellence repeated across the range of public- and private-sector institutions and corporations.

Du Gay makes the point that these institutional changes have been matched by a language of individual improvement, which invites people to engage with excellence and to exhibit '"enterprising" qualities [and] characteristics' (ibid.). Such characteristics would typically involve a willingness to take risks, to 'stand on your own feet', to innovate, to take the initiative, to compete and to challenge convention. These individualistic and profit-driven qualities are then promoted as generally achievable human virtues. The effect of all this is twofold: first, to blur the distinction 'between what is thought of as properly cultural and what is thought of as properly eco-nomic' (ibid.: 46) and, second, to blur the distinction between the individual and the organization for which he or she works. Rather than one's 'real' identity being something that exists outside the workplace, it becomes indistinguishable from one's working identity. Gramsci himself observed that people may simultaneously hold several identities, such as being a Catholic and a worker, but it took great effort on the part of the Church to hold these contradictory identities together. By linking different identities, the need for external, institutional control is lessened, and the individual manages him- or herself. Under the regime of 'Culture Excellence', du Gay notes, work is no longer a 'painful obligation', nor undertaken purely for financial gain. Instead it is 'a means of self-fulfilment, and the road to company profit is also the road to individual self-development and "growth"' (ibid.: 55).

We might ask how this identity of excellence has been disseminated. Salaman (1997) identifies a number of sites and techniques for transmitting a vision of excellence, such as training courses, assessment centres, away-days, appraisal systems and counselling procedures. These practices typically make extensive use of representations such as management guru literature and training videos. Although they may not use the term, what is striking about these strategies is their proximity to Gramscian notions of hegemony. The hearts and minds of employees are to be won not by imposing values but by expanding participation in setting goals and making decisions. He quotes one work on management theory which argues that 'companies that have been reengineered [*sic*] don't want employees who can follow rules: they want people who will make their own rules' (Salaman 1997: 256). Similarly, Terrence Deal and Allan Kennedy's (1982) evangelical work on 'corporate culture' accentuates the role of the individual in producing, rather than simply absorbing meaning:

> If employees know what their company stands for, if they know what standards they are to uphold, then they are much more likely to make decisions that will support those standards. They are also more likely to feel as if they are an important part of the organization. They are motivated because life in the company has meaning for them.
>
> (cited in Salaman 1997: 273)

This closely resembles Gramsci's invocation of the self-governing individual as the key figure within hegemonic projects (Gramsci 1971: 268). Symbolically at least, it suggests a break with 'domination' in favour of 'softer', more integrative modes of leadership. There is no guarantee, however, that these corporate culture narratives will succeed in constructing a new consensus around work. Despite their role in preparing employees 'for the way they will participate in organizations and for how they will be treated' (Salaman 1997: 253), this will fall some way short of such projects being truly 'expansive' in the sense of subaltern individuals accepting corporate values as being indistinguishable from their own. Indeed, we may be highly sceptical about the extent to which subalterns identify with corporate culture. Despite posing the question of why there is not more overt hostility to excellence initiatives, Hugh Wilmott (1997) has argued that employees typically have little deep identification with corporate values, being much more likely to distance themselves from such belief systems through cynical comments and parody. Where values *are* realized, for Wilmott, it will generally be selectively and through the employees' sense of how to maximize their rewards and minimize any possible penalties.

Gramsci does not claim that leadership is only secured through ideological means – it may also be gained through material rewards. But it is likely to be most durable amongst those groups who most readily accept its values as their own. The people that are therefore most effectively hegemonized by embodied practices and rhetorics of excellence are managers themselves. Excellence projects resonate with managers' own values: self-realization, self-presentation and self-direction are the attributes, skills and values that attracted them to management in the first place. And although a more 'de-controlled' style of leadership may diffuse authority, it is still leadership and demands implementation by managers who, as Salaman puts it, have 'dramatic and heroic status [as] transformative leaders' (1997: 330).

Treating 'new management' or excellence discourse in this way suggests it is a limited hegemonic project whose hold on subaltern consciousness is fragile. Rather than it being an expansive form of hegemony, it seems that the most effective role of such discourses is to hegemonize the hegemonic class itself – thus guaranteeing a continual stream of enterprising initiatives, but achieving no particular success within popular consciousness.

Such a view is in need of greater nuance, for two reasons. First, the category of managers has been vastly expanded over the last century. Rather than being a 'dominant' class, they are themselves an often insecure, subaltern class of salaried functionaries. The appeal of excellence is therefore not to a numerically insignificant social group but to a significant portion of middle- and even working-class workers. Second, while a fully formed 'philosophy' of excellence may be open to parody and ridicule, elements of excellence have found their way into other aspects of social life. In dialogue with other everyday practices, their ties have proved more binding. I want, therefore, to suggest some of the ways in which excellence is tied to other identities as a form of common sense and lived experience.

One direction for this is suggested by Ann Gray (2003) in her work on a group of 'enterprising women' in the organization Women in Management. Gray notes that while this group does not use the word 'feminism', 'much of what they do is underpinned by an assumed feminism' (ibid.: 504). Her project shows that excellence establishes itself as an identity of subalterns who perceive themselves as lacking the credentials to feel at home amongst the dominant bloc. An identification with excellence springs most readily and impatiently to life amongst those who feel that they have to work at success, rather than having it given to them. Gray's interviewees therefore stress that the values of excellence are aligned with the competences they possess as women. As a consequence of childcare and their traditionally insecure or part-time position within the labour market, the Women in Management group developed a flexibility that resonated with corporate imperatives. Their feminine competences in interpersonal communication, emotional literacy, self-presentation and image are now valuable skills in the marketplace and their informal knowledges, primarily acquired through consumption practices, have an immediacy and relevance that cannot be gained through formal education. For this group of women, therefore, enterprise and excellence represent a truly expansive project, one that undermines the assumed equation between masculinity and management and collapses together the fields of production and consumption, work and domesticity.

Gray therefore usefully directs our attention away from the world of work to other spaces and activities within civil society where excellent identities are being constructed. We can identify another convergence of excellence and identity within the sphere of leisure, sport and fitness. Since the 1970s, the notion of a healthy 'lifestyle' has bridged the gap between health promotion and politically motivated attempts to roll back the frontiers of welfare provision (in Gramscian terms, between 'civil society' and 'political society'). Commenting on a picture of young woman gymnast used in a campaign to promote redevelopment in the historically left-wing city of Liverpool, Colin Mercer (1984: 6) makes the point that the image 'says slim and trim after years of excess, decadence, sloppy welfarism and lazy state socialism'.

This healthy lifestyle is an effective means of conveying the ideology of excellence because it appears to be autonomous from the world of work and business. Gramsci himself anticipated such an association in an early essay on football. Showing a limited grasp of local tastes, Gramsci argued that football would never be popular in Italy because the game expressed a Northern European work ethic. Despite this misconception, his analysis acutely notes that organized sport performs a seemingly contradictory role. On the one hand, economic life is invisible within football, which offers itself as a zone of pure leisure in which the player can 'be himself'. But equally, football represents a purified image of how capitalist society could work, with each man adopting a separate, specialized role, and all players freely and happily performing to the rules of the game. Sporting conformity, which appears to originate with the worker himself, is thus actually a form of industrial management. 'Observe a game of football', Gramsci writes:

> [I]t is a model of individualistic society. It demands initiative, but an initiative which keeps within the framework of the law. Individuals are hierarchically differentiated, but differentiated on the grounds of their particular abilities, rather than their past careers. There is movement, competition, conflict, but they are regulated by an unwritten rule — the rule of fair play, of which the referee's presence is a constant reminder. The open field — air circulating freely — healthy lungs — strong muscles, always primed for action.
>
> (Gramsci 1994: 73)

Many modern fitness activities are, of course, less clearly codified than football, but the same principles apply. They appear to be independent of the world of work, while at the same time making an appeal to individuals as being physically self-reliant — a message that has a particular appeal to the subaltern middle class, amongst whom the cultivation of the body as a life project is most widespread and deeply rooted (Bourdieu 1997: 112). The struggle for leadership is therefore taking place in a language and set of practices that appear to be autonomous of broader economic and political implications. As Jeremy Howell and Alan Ingham (2001: 346) point out, this 'is a struggle couched in a politically innocuous language — lifestyle management — and self-improvement policies that leave most of us saying

"What fool would argue with that?"'. It is this taken-for-grantedness that aligns excellence with Gramscian common sense.

It is important to realize that incorporative projects like Women in Management or the boom in fitness and lifestyle do not attract everyone. Identities are formed in opposition to other identities. To identify with excellence is to assume that there are others who stand outside this order and who must be 'dominated'. As du Gay (1997) notes, because all people are now individualized as potential self-starters and risk-takers, those who 'fail', such as the homeless, the unemployed or the unfit, are subject to intensive disapproval. Because these people are now represented as having 'a moral duty to take care of themselves, they can blame no one but themselves for the problems they face' (du Gay 1997: 302). Similarly, Howell and Ingham note that 'the darker side of the sunny "Help Yourself to Health" view of life is that the status of illness and health is beginning to shift from an item of bad luck to a vice' (ibid.: 338). 'Excellence' therefore involves the construction of a morally and intellectually 'dominated' group outside the hegemonic bloc. But it is not only the leading social group who are in the position to construct such an identity, and it is to this issue that we now turn.

YOUTH SUBCULTURES

We have seen that hegemonic blocs typically draw sharp distinctions between subalterns, who must be accommodated within the bloc, and adversaries who constitute a threat to it. In this regard, Gramsci's distinction between subalterns and the dominated resembles the anthropologist Mary Douglas's view of culture. For Douglas (1966), cultural order involves a set of classifications about what is properly inside a system, and the threats that lie outside it, with the boundary between the two being tenaciously – if not always effectively – policed. In the next chapter we shall see how adversaries are policed, and dispensed with, through fictional representations. Here, however, we look at a range of academic literature on youth subcultures, in order to draw some conclusions about the ways in which young people come to 'own' their status as outsiders and also how such dominated groups patrol and constitute the boundaries of the hegemonic bloc itself.

The literature under review appeared in Britain at around the same time as Gramsci's ideas were being widely disseminated in translation. Gramsci's central concern with the organization of consent provided a language through which to understand the responses of young people to the protracted period of political and social consensus in Britain that followed the Second World

War. Despite pervasive claims that this era involved a lessening of class distinctions, it was clear that major class inequalities continued to be an important source of friction within British society. For the sociologist Phil Cohen, the period involved a crucial *destabilization* of the relatively affluent and influential working-class stratum he calls the 'respectables'. This class fraction was being altered by a series of competing innovations and demands: automation was replacing the skilled and semi-skilled jobs they traditionally occupied, while at the same time they were subject to appeals from government and advertisers to participate in a more middle-class, suburban lifestyle. While on the surface subcultures acted out a rejection of their parents' values, for Cohen this rejection was actually a displaced argument with class society. In a famous quote he argues that the function of a subculture is:

> To express and resolve, albeit 'magically', the contradictions which remain hidden or unresolved in the parent culture. The succession of subcultures which this parent culture generated can thus all be considered so many variations on a central theme – the contradiction, at an ideological level, between traditional working-class Puritanism and the new hedonism of consumption.

> (Cohen 1980: 82)

Subcultural resistance was a 'magical' resolution because it avoided the real conditions that were changing working-class life. Instead it involved an *oblique* form of engagement, in which (primarily) young men came to live their dominated class position as an identity and as a source of pleasure. In this way, domination involves the consent of the dominated every bit as much as moral and intellectual leadership involves the consent of subalterns. Using the example of skinhead football fans in the East End of London, Cohen argues that their identity focused around a local tribalism. In this situation, conflicts with the 'real' enemy – capitalist developers and an insensitive local state – were displaced not only onto conflict with the older generation and other subcultures, but also onto fierce antagonism towards youths from neighbouring streets and districts. This is not, writes Cohen, a total mis-understanding of their position as a dominated class. Instead, 'It is a way of retrieving the solidarities of the traditional neighbourhood destroyed by development' (ibid.: 85). Whatever resistant potential youth culture might have is therefore diverted into an extreme form of 'corporatism' which prevents any kind of alliance being formed across local differences.

If it were simply the case that youth subcultures were engaged in arguments amongst themselves, however, it would be difficult to explain the intense society-wide panics about lawless youth discussed in Key Idea 7. Youth subcultures do indeed engage in argument with the wider culture, though the extent to which they can form a truly counter-hegemonic programme is limited by their modes of expression. I wish therefore at this point to introduce the work of Dick Hebdige and Paul Willis, two authors who have discussed subcultural youths' recognition of their domination and the limitations of their resistance.

Although notions of hegemony are central to Hebdige's work, he reconceives it as a matter not just of political negotiation and conflict, but also of signification. Fashions, music, objects and images are the means through which dominated groups express their unwillingness to be organized into the dominant order. 'The challenge to hegemony which subcultures represent', he writes, 'is not issued directly by them. Rather it is expressed obliquely, in style' (Hebdige: 1979: 16). Leaving aside the questionable assertions that subcultures involve no direct challenge to the dominant bloc (think of the politicized rhetoric of some popular music) and lie beneath the consciousness of individual members of a subculture, Hebdige effectively demonstrates the everyday nature of hegemonic struggle. Just as the dominant bloc's verbal appeal to its subalterns may be turned against it (think of words such as 'freedom' or 'equality'), so the material culture of mainstream society is, for Hebdige, appropriated by subcultures as an act of subversion. Thus, the narcissistic style of the 1960s mod subculture transformed the 'straight' meanings of a suit, a scooter or a neat haircut 'into an offensive weapon' (ibid.: 104). Such actions are a refusal of a hegemonic project's claims to speak for all people. The use of style in subcultures interrupts the process of 'normalization'. These tactics, he writes, 'are gestures, movements towards a speech which offends the "silent majority", which challenges the principle of unity and cohesion, which contradicts the myth of consensus' (ibid.: 18).

Hebdige is at pains to emphasize that this is an expansive resistance or counter-hegemony since it involves making emotional and stylistic alliances with other groups, notably immigrants from the Caribbean. However, a problem with his argument lies precisely in its focus on style. Revolts through style may be initially shocking to 'straight' society but they are also readily co-opted by capitalist fashion and art systems. Rather than fundamentally altering the dominated position of working-class and black youth, their role might be better conceived of as redefining the limits of acceptability in mainstream society. Moreover, despite his attempts to categorize subcultural counter-hegemony as expansive, his concentration on a minority of 'spectacular' young people rests on the idea of a stylistic avant-garde who are autonomous of the mass of youth. As we shall see in key idea 6, this avant-gardism sits uncomfortably with Gramsci's notion of leadership.

We can find a similar sense of a limited counter-hegemonic project in the work of Paul Willis, whose *Learning to Labour* (1977) examines the role of working-class culture, and particularly the 'counter-school culture' of secondary education in shaping working-class boys' expectations about their future in the world of work. 'The most difficult thing to explain about working-class kids', he argues, 'is why they allow themselves to get working-class jobs' (Willis 1977: 1). The answer to this question, for Willis, lies in the way they claim a dominated identity for themselves by recasting their subordinated status as something else, 'as true learning, affirmation, appropriation and as a form of resistance' (ibid.: 3). In a mirror image of the expansive moment of hegemony, the most disruptive group of boys (who Willis calls 'the lads') seize their domination as an expression of their real interests.

The 'lads' resistance', which takes the form of a 'caged resentment, [always stopping] just short of outright confrontation' (ibid.: 12–13), is both a consequence and a cause of their seeing through the rhetoric of teaching. Politicians, teachers and parents may believe that all pupils, regardless of their class, are receiving an inherently useful education. But the school essentially teaches children how to be good workers by mimicking the division of labour in a factory. Within the school, teachers are powerful and the 'good' pupil is the one who learns to conform to this unequal distribution of authority. The 'lads', however, differentiate themselves from this teaching paradigm, creating for themselves a posture of joking macho defiance which, it so happens, is exactly the indifferent posture they subsequently take into the world of manual labour. Their resistance therefore ultimately turns out to be functional to capitalism, though Willis holds out the hope that without such creativity and inventiveness, no counter-hegemonic project could be successful.

One of the reasons the 'lads' are unable to fully articulate a counter-hegemony is because they are not simply a dominated class, but also dominators when seen through the prism of gender, sexuality and race:

The 'tragedy' of their situation is that [their] forms of 'penetration' are limited, distorted and twisted back on themselves, often unintentionally, by

... the widespread influence of a form of patriarchal male domination and sexism within working class culture itself.

(Willis 1977: 3)

Learning to Labour has been criticized for its perfunctory address to this sexism, and for the veil it draws over the overt racism and homophobia of the 'lads' (Skeggs 1992). But even this minimal consideration points us towards a problem with thinking about oppositional identities: what is subordinate in one register may well be hegemonic (or dominant) in another. In thinking about the play of hegemony, domination and resistance, we therefore need to be aware of the different forms taken by power, and that the identity of the dominant bloc itself is not something entirely unified and unchanging, but a composite of multiple, and often contradictory, identities. We consider this further in the chapter 'After Gramsci'.

The last two sections have shown that the identity of neither subalterns nor the dominated can be ideologically imposed upon them. Instead they must reach up to claim it, and this will involve linking the hegemonic project with common-sense understandings of the world. What distinguishes hegemonic theory from functionalism (the idea that all aspects of society work towards social cohesion) is that this will reflexively alter the shape of the hegemonic bloc itself, as it is forced to respond to the aspirations of its subalterns. We move on in the next chapter to look at how this give-and-take is also acted out symbolically, and within the institutions of culture.

5

HEGEMONY IN PRACTICE 2: REPRESENTATIONS AND INSTITUTIONS

NARRATIVES OF AUTHORITY

As we saw in the preceding chapter, the production of identities is at least partly achieved through the circulation of images and texts that promote or reject particular subject positions. Gramsci was himself interested in the role of representation in producing a worldview, though his critical insights were largely limited to literature rather than the prominent forms of mass entertainment of his era such as film and dance music. Here we shall concern ourselves with mainstream fictional representations, looking at the ways in which they negotiate with spectators, offering symbolic concessions to subaltern groups. Negotiation, however, is not the only strategy open to texts within the struggle for hegemony. Other texts attempt to reach into the culture of subalterns in order to fashion an image of the dominant bloc as speaking in the name of, or making common cause with, those it rules. Still others fashion their resistance at a textual level, offering symbolic resolutions to problems that are intractable in everyday life.

I emphasize that these are mainstream fictions because the Gramscian tradition breaks with earlier conceptions of how domination and resistance operate within representation. A prominent strand within textual studies has argued that cultural forms such as the novel and the film are so deeply immersed, both formally and institutionally, within capitalist, racist, patri-archal and heterosexist structures that they inevitably depict the world in ways that reproduce and thereby maintain these inequalities. Opposition can only take the form of texts that are produced outside the mainstream, whether they are 'folk' styles that predate mass cultural forms, or avant-garde texts that break with the formal and ideological conventions of dominant representation. A hegemonic understanding of the action of texts rejects both these propositions. How could a popular film, song or novel that simply reproduced the worldview of a dominant social group ever hope to live in the imaginations of its subalterns? And how could folkloric or avant-garde texts ever be sufficiently expansive to form the basis of counter-hegemony? Taking a Gramscian approach involves neither celebrating nor condemning popular texts. Instead it examines how they are produced 'in relation to the struggles between dominant and subordinate groups' (Willis 1995: 180).

In the next section we shall look at some texts that attempt to summon subaltern and subordinate groups, but this section analyses representations that assert the validity of the dominant bloc and attempt to expand its rule into a 'national-popular'. The two examples come from the cinematic action-thriller genre and involve the re-production of white masculinity. The first, brief but hard-edged, is Andrew Ross's essay on the 'Great White Dude' (1995). Here the argument is less that dominant powers negotiate with their subalterns than that they appropriate the idiom of subalternity within popular texts. Ross analyses *On Deadly Ground* (1994), a film in which Steven Seagal plays an oil rig fire-fighter battling against a crooked petrol corporation. At the climax of the film, Seagal (whose character name is, appropriately, Forrest) breaks into a long speech to an audience of Inuit, in which he outlines the horrors of environmental destruction and the need for 'the people' to reclaim the Earth from polluting corporations.

Ross's analysis of this scene shows how environmentalism, widely imagined as a counter-cultural or counter-hegemonic movement, is 'canni-balized' within reactionary popular fictions. *On Deadly Ground* reinflects the meaning of environmental politics by tying it to two other issues. The first is an American tradition of libertarianism which conflates big business and the state, such that any encroachment on individual liberty is treated as a call to arms. The second is the issue of white masculinity. Ross argues that environmentalism is a rare cause in which white men may celebrate a 'redneck' identity involving muscular endeavour within and against nature. Environmentalism, he argues, is 'one place on the map of progressive politics where the Great White Dude can hang his hat, while indulging in the wilderness cults traditionally associated with the making of heroic white, male identities' (Ross 1995: 174).

Ross captures that moment when part of the dominant bloc (indeed, the dead centre of the bloc) is forced to reposition itself. While this is a defensive reaction, it takes the form of an aggressive reclaiming of the meanings of nationhood and gendered identity. We can see a similar response to changing times in a more sustained analysis of a popular hero's appeal. Tony Bennett and Janet Woollacott's *Bond and Beyond* (1987) argues that the James Bond narratives have provided a highly adaptable and condensed means of linking diverse political and social issues. These include Britain's status after the loss of its empire, the struggles between capitalism and communism, and relations between the sexes. Bennett and Woollacott argue that this linking (what Gramsci calls the 'suture') of disparate phenomena does not impose a dominant ideology but articulates subordinate and dominant ideologies together, 'overlapping them onto one another so as to bring about move-ments and reformations of subjectivity' (ibid.: 235).

Bennett and Woollacott make it clear that Bond was not initially a popular hero. His creator, Ian Fleming, and the publishers Jonathan Cape saw him having an ironic appeal for a readership drawn from the metropolitan literary intelligentsia. However, serialization of *From Russia, With Love* in the middle-brow *Daily Express* newspaper in 1957 widened the fiction's appeal. *From Russia, With Love* appeared to be more clearly grounded in the political landscape than Fleming's other novels and Bond's defeat of maverick Soviet agents in the novel 'embodied the imaginary possibility that England might once again be placed at the centre of world affairs' (ibid.: 26). This had a particular appeal at a time when Britain's empire was rapidly disappearing and its international influence dwindling.

Bond's appearance in film further broadened his appeal in Britain but also made him a popular hero internationally. These twin developments led to an adaptation in both the character of Bond himself and in the films' recurrent motifs. Bennett and Woollacott note that the choice of a working-class Scot, Sean Connery, to play Bond symbolized Britain as a modern and 'classless' nation at odds with the upper-class paternalism represented by Bond's superiors. The 'Bond Girl' of the films represented a similar spirit of modernization, since her independent sexuality was 'liberated from the constraints of family, marriage and domesticity' (ibid.: 35). Bennett and Woollacott see this shift as evidence of the flexible nature of popular fictions within the hegemonic process. For while the limited Bond of the 1950s was one who could symbolically refurbish a sense of imperialist self-importance, the tough, professional and insubordinate Bond of the 1960s was 'a hero of rupture *and* tradition', one who could link a technological and meritocratic future with folk memories of an independent and pioneering past, playing both ends off against a restrictive and repressed Establishment.

Already, then, we have some sense of how texts negotiate with their audiences, though this is not to suggest that popular feeling is always modernizing, progressive or liberating. Bennett and Woollacott identify a later 'moment of Bond' in which the films' international politics became deeply chauvinistic, and their representations of gender worked to symbolically undermine the gains of feminism. We might ask why the Bond fictions had to periodically reinvent themselves over this period (and subsequently – you might wish to think about the transformations of more recent Bond films). Bennett and Woollacott's answer is that, between the 1950s and 1980s, traditional modes of leadership had been placed in doubt and new alternatives were not yet fully formed. In such a situation fictional representations were able to offer a quicker response than the institutions of political society. In the case of Bond, this was a conservative response, 'filling the gaps in other practices in producing consent' (ibid.: 282). Popular fiction, Bennett and Woollacott argue, 'is more closely in touch with popular sentiment, quicker to register when specific ideological combinations are losing their "pulling power"' and better able to make the 'ideological adjustments' in popular taste that can suture 'the people' back into a new hegemonic equilibrium.

We have seen, therefore, how texts have a role to play in the dominant bloc's attempt to reshape itself in the hope of winning popular support for its rule. But how does it address 'the people' themselves? And is there a possibility of texts showing resistance to the threat of incorporation? We consider these issues below.

NEGOTIATION AND RESISTANCE

In this section we take the idea of textual negotiation further by analysing three films that grant rather more in the way of concession than the Bond cycle. We then move on to think about the possibilities of counter-hegemony through the analysis of texts whose stance is more clearly oppositional.

Some of the most productive work on textual negotiation has been that which reads multiple social relations such as class, race and/or gender together. One such is Judith Williamson's (1991) study of Hollywood images of big business. Williamson argues that despite their economic success, capitalist corporations have failed to establish any emotional resonance with 'the people' and therefore appear cold and remote. Films Like *Trading Places* (1983) and *Working Girl* (1988) attempt to reconcile capitalism and popular aspirations and to challenge the ways that capitalism does business. In *Trading Places*, the billionaire Duke Brothers engineer a life-swap between Billy-Ray Valentine (Eddie Murphy), a black hustler, and their white stockbroker nephew Winthorpe (Dan Aykroyd). For its first half the film revels in images of Billy-Ray's financial acumen, as he uses his street-learned good sense to make profits for himself and the Dukes. This upward mobility is counter-posed to scenes of Winthorpe being reduced to poverty as the symbols of his privileged white identity are stripped away. However, when the Dukes' double-dealing and racism is exposed in the second half of the film, Billy-Ray and Winthorpe join forces to ruin the brothers and make a fortune for themselves. The text therefore 'works' by mapping the two protagonists' values onto one another. Williamson describes Billy-Ray as embodying ideals of 'enterprise' and Winthorpe 'heritage'. These values are articulated together since 'when enterprise seems greedy and cut-throat, heritage can provide *noblesse oblige*; but when heritage appears snobbish and unjust, enterprise can be meritocratic and open' (ibid.: 157).

Like Billy-Ray, Tess McGill (Melanie Griffith), the heroine of *Working Girl*, is a disadvantaged 'natural' who makes use of her good sense and knowledge of popular culture to escape from the typing pool to a senior position in a large corporation. In the course of this transformation, she is regularly humiliated and betrayed by her boss Katherine (Sigourney Weaver), another privileged insider, until Katherine is finally unmasked as a cheat and dismissed. Just as we saw in the earlier discussion of 'excellence', the binding ties of the text are produced by suggesting that the values of finance capitalism within the film are not, ultimately, distinct from Tess's human qualities as a working-class woman. For capitalism to succeed, it must incorporate Tess's ethic of courage, commitment and honesty. Williamson points to the extraordinary final sequence of the film in which Tess is illuminated within a Manhattan skyscraper with the title track, Carly Simon's 'New Jerusalem' swelling behind the image. 'Rising "up where you belong"', she notes, 'can have at once profoundly spiritual and totally material connotations: it involves social betterment . . . *and* a sense of "higher" values, or ethics beyond simple greed' (ibid.: 160).

This sense of negotiation is shared by a very different 'women's film'. *Millions Like Us* (1943) was made during the Second World War at the behest of the British government's propaganda department, the Ministry of

Information. While we might imagine that coercive measures take prece-
dence over negotiation during wartime, the need to mobilize citizens for a
war effort clearly involves winning the consent of subordinates. This was
accentuated by the particular conditions that faced Britain at the outbreak of
the Second World War. Memories of the First World War, the austere
conditions of the interwar years and ineffective early attempts at propaganda
meant that the war was not, initially, a popular one. It therefore became a
necessity to bridge the gap between government and people, to insist within
representation that it was a 'People's War' fought by both sexes, whose
outcome would be not just the defeat of Germany but also a transformation
of Britain. As Geoff Hurd (1984: 18) puts it, 'The war created an urgent need
to convert dominance into hegemony, requiring a rapid and genuine response
to the aspirations of subordinate groups and classes.' Above all, these
aspirations involved a postwar future in which demands for greater equality
and social justice would be met.

Individual texts, however, negotiate this progressive sense of the national-
popular, mixing elements of what Raymond Williams (1980) calls the
'emergent' with images of 'dominant' social inequality. Thus, while the
specific focus of *Millions Like Us* is the need for women war workers, the text
treats this as a temporary measure only. Tensions between the short-term
need for women's labour and longer-term changes in relations between the
classes and genders are discussed and resolved within the narrative.

Two plotlines are central to this. One concerns Celia (Patricia Roc), a
lower-class girl who is conscripted into the workforce. After initial misgiv-
ings about the lack of glamour associated with industrial labour, she finds
herself welcomed into a classless community of women. Prone to romantic
daydreaming, Celia marries an airman, but when he is killed in action she
is reincorporated into the surrogate family of women, her acceptance of
the need to serve the nation underscored by the film's final shot of her join-
ing in with a popular song. The other storyline deals with Jennifer (Ann
Crawford), a rich and snobbish girl who provides a means for the film to deal
with the ruling class. Throughout much of the film she is shown to be inferior
to her lower-class workmates, both in her skills on the lathe and in her values.
Nonetheless, she enjoys a romance with the brusque foreman of the factory,
Charlie (Eric Portman). Late in the film, Charlie is given one of its key
progressive speeches, in which he points out that their love is dependent
upon a temporary cessation of class hostility. 'What's going to happen when
it's all over?' he asks. 'Shall we go on like this or shall we slide back – that's
what I want to know. I'm not marrying you, Jenny, until I'm sure.'

In terms of class, therefore, progressive values seem to have the last word. But as Andrew Higson (1995) argues, the film reproduces a series of dominant gender inequalities. The women are constantly supervised by men, and above the foremen is a state that controls their actions but which remains relatively invisible. Moreover, the film operates within a set of restrictive moral codes: both Celia and Jennifer desire a future within the patriarchal family, and the non-patriarchal 'family' of the women workers is one that demands the renunciation of sexual or romantic desire. As Higson comments, this calls into question the extent to which real textual concessions are made. The characters at the centre of the narrative show no desire for change, and while *Millions Like Us* depends 'on the narrative centrality of ordinary people, working people – it is a respectable, lower middle-class position which is finally privileged within the social formation of ordinary people' (ibid.: 243).

So far, then, we have seen how the authority of the leading bloc is *maintained* within representations, despite the negotiations and concessions they must make. But other texts offer a clearer challenge to the dominant bloc than this, and aim to fundamentally shift values and beliefs. Where then can we find evidence of a counter-hegemony being assembled in representation?

One of the most sustained hegemonic analyses of a resistant mode is Tricia Rose's study of hip-hop, *Black Noise* (1994). Rose argues that resistance originates outside a public culture that is saturated with the values and strategies of the dominant. Instead, it takes the form of disguised or coded cultural practices 'that invert stigmas, direct our attention to offstage cultures of the class or group within which they originated, and validate the perceptions of the less powerful' (Rose 1994: 100). Rap's musical rage at the injuries inflicted on African-Americans is of a form that she terms the 'hidden transcript'. However, the extent to which rap can remain truly hidden within a capitalist music industry that distributes 'authentic' forms of expression globally, profits from them and neutralizes their political content, is open to question. Rap therefore exists in the space between the hidden and public domains, 'making [its protests] highly visible, yet difficult to contain and confine' (ibid.: 101). Like Bennett and Woollacott's analysis of popular fictions, rap is well positioned to respond quickly to cultural change, keeping it one step ahead of more slow-moving institutional changes. 'As new ideological fissures and points of contradiction develop', she writes, 'new mutts bark and growl, and new dogcatchers are dispatched' (ibid.: 102).

Rose's argument suggests some of the problems that we have already encountered in thinking about the possibilities of counter-hegemony. While rap makes expansive connections amongst the people of the African diaspora, and across racial boundaries, its resistive potential is limited by the sexism, homophobia and anti-Semitism of some rap artists' lyrics. Rose therefore considers women rappers as a group on the margins of an already marginalized cultural product. Perhaps here we can find a pure form of resistance? Indeed, the niche that they have carved out for themselves, she argues, is one that resists 'patterns of sexual objectification at the hands of black men and cultural invisibility at the hands of the dominant American culture' (ibid.: 170). Yet this is not a totalizing act of resistance. Rose notes that these rappers are wary of feminism, a political project which, for them, is associated with white femininity. What might at first seem a pure space of opposition to 'dominant' racist and sexist ideologies is, for Rose, better seen as a difficult and shifting dialogue between women rappers, black machismo and white feminism.

Using Rose's study as a limit case of subordinate cultural production, it should be clear that it is very difficult to conceptualize some pure moment of 'resistance' within a Gramscian framework, since the identities and representational forms of the dominated are formed through an engagement with the hegemonic projects of the power bloc. This is not the same as a cultural pessimism, which contends that subaltern groups are entirely hegemonized within the dominant bloc, and other voices 'liquidated'. Those other voices are audible through their dialogue with the expressive practices of the dominant group. Writing about Caribbean popular culture, Stuart Hall has noted the difficulties of entirely 'refusing' imperial representations of island life since they are partly constitutive – even as a jumping-off point – of Caribbean identity. Who, he writes, 'could describe this tense and tortured dialogue as a "one way trip"?' (Hall 1990: 235).

INSTITUTIONAL HEGEMONY

In this section we look at an issue that has been addressed haphazardly throughout the chapter. Hammertown School, Women in Management, the music industry and the Ministry of Information are all institutions that work to transmit sets of values. However, these values are not identical with a 'dominant ideology'. The fact that institutions have specific forms of organization and practice means that they cannot pass on values in a friction-less way, as a syringe would inject a liquid into a vein. Instead they *mediate* between the ruling group and its intended audience. While institutions may well be vital tools of the power bloc, they typically produce a set of values that are negotiated through their own circumstances and traditions. The example I shall use to illustrate this is an institution we encountered earlier, the BBC. By looking at a recent moment in the BBC's history, we can see some of the frictions that occur between an institution, the state and the public.

Although the BBC in some ways functions as the state broadcaster in Britain (it is state-funded through a compulsory licence fee), it does not always transmit news stories that are favourable to the government of the day. Its interrogation of the military intelligence used to justify the US-led coalition's invasion of Iraq in 2003, for instance, led to direct and serious conflict both with the Labour government and with those media bodies that supported the war. Although these events focused on the suicide of a government scientist, Dr David Kelly, they took place within a wider context of discussions over the ten-yearly renewal of the BBC's Charter. The results of these discussions were published in 2005, and asked questions of the BBC's status as an institution (for example, the fact that it straddles commercial and public service activities, and that it is essentially self-regulating).

In terms of hegemony, we can draw several issues from this episode. First, the incident suggests that Gramsci's thoughts on the separation of civil and political society need to be revised. We may remember that Gramsci distinguishes between 'the ensemble of organisms commonly called "private"' (civil society) and a coercive state ('political society'), maintaining that hegemony needs to be won first within civil society. Yet not only does the state have a greatly expanded role in modern societies (and a more limited coercive role) but the boundary between the state and commerce has become increasingly porous, with state institutions being required to seek non-state income sources such as corporate sponsorship, private investment and profitable ventures of its own. The BBC has a *'state' role* as Britain's official broadcaster (through, for example, the BBC World Service), a *'private' role* as the commissioner, producer and broadcaster of entertainment programmes which construct the meanings of privacy within British society, and a *commercial role* through its publishing and overseas activities.

Second, the incident indicated that institutions have a high level of autonomy. It is a structural feature of 'mature' democracies that institutions such as political parties, media organizations, business corporations and religious bodies have distinctive interests which generate disagreements. These differences are not trivial or illusory, though the terms of the conflict are sufficiently limited that they cannot 'touch the essential' by calling capitalist democracy itself into question. Instead, what Gramsci calls the 'discordant *ensemble* of the superstructures' legitimates the social structure by demonstrating its capacity for self-criticism and limited change. What made the Kelly Affair particularly noteworthy was that the Labour government risked this legitimacy by attempting to assert its authority over the BBC through legal-coercive measures.

Third, institutions compete with one another to speak to, and on behalf of, 'the people'. Elspeth Probyn (2000), for example, has analysed the continuing popularity of McDonald's in the face of counter-hegemonic critiques of its business practices. She sees the corporation as having constructed an image of itself which speaks directly to its consumers, establishing a bond between its corporate values and those of families. McDonald's advertising, she argues, makes links between the family that eats together and a 'global family', thereby 'extending an ethics of care into the realm of global capitalism and creating its customer as a globalised familial citizen' (ibid.: 35). Similarly, criticism of the BBC's Charter renewal focused on its populist programming. It was argued that the BBC's role is to produce 'quality' (high- and middle-brow) radio and television, whereas the policy of successive Directors-General has been to appeal to popular taste. To concentrate on quality programming would be to jeopardize its position as a genuinely 'national-popular' institution. The BBC, like other intermediate institutions, was therefore caught between the competing needs to satisfy a higher power and to make its own popular appeal.

Fourth, institutions are to some extent an assemblage of agents or, as we shall see in the following chapter, 'intellectuals'. Although there is a BBC structure and ethos, it is also a collection of individuals and teams – and, indeed, much of the coverage of the Kelly Affair focused on one journalist, Andrew Gilligan. Institutions do not automatically speak with one voice and there is potential for friction and negotiation between individuals and corporate structures and traditions. In the context of another culture industry, cinema, Christine Gledhill (1988) has argued that 'creative' personnel operate within different professional and aesthetic frameworks from their companies and shareholders, and this may result in ideological conflict. 'Such conflict', she remarks, 'is, indeed, part of the ideology of creativity itself' (ibid.: 69). We do not, however, need to limit ourselves to media institutions – any institution is likely to involve such transactions, and there are few examples of an institution that does not rely on some degree of potentially conflictual agency or initiative from its members.

Finally, institutions are increasingly global. During the Kelly Affair, the most vociferous objections to both the BBC's reporting and its licence renewal came from Rupert Murdoch's multinational News Corporation, which has a variety of press and television interests in the UK. While the episode could be framed as a largely 'national' one, inasmuch as it was focused on the British government, the opposition between the BBC and News Corporation indicated that media institutions are increasingly bound up in a transnational media system in which national broadcasters compete with global (and particularly American) networks in order to make their popular appeals. That there has been a displacement of national hegemonic projects by international ones is suggested by Shaun Moores' study of satellite television in which one interviewee comments:

> 'With the BBC, you always feel as though the structure of society is there, the authority. Their newsreaders speak just like schoolmasters. They're telling you, like schoolmasters telling the kids. I think Sky News has more of a North American approach, it's more relaxed. They treat you like equals and don't take the audience for a bunch of small kids.'
>
> (Moores 2000: 80)

We shall return to this issue in the chapter on 'Americanism and Fordism'.

SUMMARY

The last two chapters have shown that the struggle for hegemony takes place across the full range of social practices – within consumption, production, identity, regulation and representation. They have stressed that hegemony is a reflexive process in which the values of the power bloc, subalterns and counter-hegemonic forces are in a constant state of negotiation, compromise and change. I end with a question. Dominic Strinati (1995) argues that hegemony is finally pessimistic because it is, above all, a theory of how power is retained. Do you accept this? Or do you lean towards the position that hegemony is fundamentally optimistic since it holds that however strong a leading bloc seems, its need to live in the hearts and minds of those it rules will ultimately corrode it, and its oppressive power will finally falter and fail?

6

INTELLECTUALS

THE 'PROBLEM OF THE INTELLECTUALS'

This chapter considers the role of intellectuals in giving form and expression to the moral, philosophical, ideological and scientific values that are elaborated into a hegemonic project. The chapter again works through examples to give a sense of how values cohere around the figure of the intellectual and how such meanings are contested between groups of intellectuals, and between the intelligentsia and the publics they labour to hegemonize. Intellectuals introduce a dimension of agency to the hegemonic process that may appear to be absent in more impersonal phenomena such as texts and institutions. However, we should be cautious when distinguishing between these categories, or when placing an accent upon agency. In the previous chapter we saw that institutions can be thought of as networks of agents. Intellectuals work within institutions, and institutions require intellectuals with the specific skills needed to maintain the institution theoretically. Similarly, intellectuals may produce representations, but the image of the intellectual, whether as disinterested authority or as engaged thinker, is one that is constructed within representation.

Nor should we overestimate the extent to which Gramsci privileges agency over structure, as criticisms of his work sometimes imply. His starting point is famously that 'all men are intellectuals', but he qualifies this by arguing that only a minority of people can function as intellectuals within any given society. By this he means that there is no particular characteristic that unifies intellectual activities as opposed to practical ones, since manual tasks also have a creative and thinking dimension. Instead, the meaning of being an intellectual is generated by the 'complex [or structure] of social relations' at a historical moment, within which some practices are privileged as being intellectual, while others are relegated to the status of common sense or practical knowledge. So, while art has been an intellectual activity for some centuries, until the twentieth century design was relegated to the position of practical knowledge (both would now be seen as intellectual activities with appropriate certification). Cooking and eating have generally been seen as mundane and practical activities, but they now have an expanded category of culinary intellectuals – TV chefs, journalists, restaurateurs, nutritionists and so on – who mediate between food producers and the public, confirming the rightness or otherwise of a person's taste choices.

Being an intellectual is therefore to some extent predicated on the productive requirements of capitalism in a period, although intellectuals will reflexively shape the character of production and are themselves entrepreneurs and producers (of ideas, texts, modes of organization and so on). Gramsci further undermines the notion of intellectuals as free-floating isolated thinkers, by gesturing towards the idea of a 'collective intellectual'. By this he means the revolutionary party, but we could think of other institutions and groupings that 'think' collectively – financial elites, artistic and subcultural avant-gardes, media corporations and so on. Intellectuals, then, are certainly agents, but there is also an intellectual structure within society.

We might ask why Gramsci was so concerned with intellectuals (indeed, his original plan was that the *Prison Notebooks* would be a history of Italian intellectuals). The answer lies in the problem of political representation: in other words, who is entitled to speak and think on behalf of a particular constituency? Like many other socialist intellectuals, Gramsci was a disaffected bourgeois who aligned himself with the working class. Socialism was Gramsci's decision, and not something 'given' by his class position (to prove the point, one of his brothers became a Fascist). Despite the hardship of his childhood and the years in Turin, he did not belong to the working class and the effort to bridge the gap between university-educated Communists and factory workers proved largely unsuccessful. After the failure of a 'proletarian university' during the 1920 Fiat factory take-over, he noted that it had proved impossible 'to get beyond the limited group, the closed circle, the efforts of a few isolated individuals' (Gramsci 1994: 226.)

The distance between middle-class intellectuals and the working class was a persistent problem for revolutionary socialism. Once again Lenin's thoughts on the subject provided Gramsci with both inspiration and a point of departure. For Lenin, the Russian intelligentsia of the nineteenth century was worryingly detached from the working class on whose behalf they formulated a theory of revolution. 'In Russia', he wrote, 'the theory of Social-Democracy arose independently of the spontaneous growth of the labour movement; it arose as [the] outcome of ideas among the revolutionary socialist intelligentsia' (cited in Hill 1947: 68). Marxism could only be brought into the labour movement 'from without', yet the intellectuals could not be allowed to dominate the movement. Lenin's vehicle for overcoming this impasse was the Revolutionary Party, which would fuse former workers and former intellectuals into a single, disciplined organism whose members would be 'professional revolutionaries'. Rather than seeing the Party as a mass movement, Lenin advocates the development of a vanguard or elite that will impose socialist consciousness on the masses. It will achieve this through its monopoly of the state's coercive apparatuses, which it has seized during the overthrow of the previous regime. After a period of proletarian dictatorship, class differences will disappear, and the distinction between workers and intellectuals will 'be obliterated'. It is open to question whether this dissolution of boundaries took place in Soviet Russia, where a pervasive communist bureaucracy was quickly established. Certainly many intellectuals, workers and peasants were literally obliterated in the attempt.

What Gramsci took from Lenin was primarily the notion that the intellectuals, the working class and the peasantry need to be fused in some way. For that to be successful in the long term, the working class must develop its own theoreticians, to whom he gives the name *organic* intellectuals. The remainder of this chapter considers how we may apply this idea in order to distinguish between intellectuals who are organic to a social group and the superseded intelligentsia, which he terms *traditional* intellectuals. The chapter evaluates the extent to which this opposition is sustainable, since, as Gramsci acknowledges, intellectuals may fulfil both organic and traditional functions.

This dynamic view of organic and traditional intellectuals is just one way in which Gramsci's flexible Marxism transcends Lenin's somewhat 'top-down' account of how ideas are transmitted. Since the transformation of civil society is a precondition of radical social change for Gramsci, intellectuals must shape their world through consent rather than though imposing their ideas. The logic of Gramsci's argument therefore points away from vanguardism and towards the development of a genuinely mass form of intellectual life. As with hegemony more generally, Gramsci sees intellectual life as a form of negotiation. Emerging forms of thought (such as socialism) encounter existing intellectual forms, both those of previous ruling groups and the common sense of working people, and are shaped into 'a momentary equilibrium' with them. There is nothing guaranteed about this: the battle of ideas may be slow or end in defeat.

While this introduction has dealt largely with the intellectual as a political theoretician, the remainder of the chapter will once again blur the boundaries between different areas of social life. For, as I noted at the beginning of the chapter, 'intellectual life' in any period is an elaboration of discrete elements that include politics, artistic production, science and morality (though one or more of these might give a period its particular character). Political activists, producers of popular culture, style leaders and business elites are therefore deployed as case studies of the intelligentsia. For the moment, however, we shall return to Gramsci's central binary opposition.

ORGANIC INTELLECTUALS

Gramsci argues that 'every social group, coming into existence . . . creates together with itself, organically, one or more strata of intellectuals' (1971: 5). While in orthodox Marxist fashion he sees these 'social groups' (or classes) as fulfilling a function within economic production, we need not apply this observation exclusively in class terms. It was, for example, integral to the development of a politicized black identity, above all in America, that this emergence was theorized and represented by black intellectuals. Similarly, political movements around women's liberation, gay rights and environmentalism are strongly associated with the intellectuals who work to give them 'homogeneity and an awareness of [their] function . . . in the economic . . . social and political fields' (ibid.) Nonetheless, what distinguishes class politics from these other movements is the extent to which production, with its specific legal, organizational, scientific and technological requirements, is of central concern. Gramsci notes that the development of capitalism was accompanied by the growth of new types of intellectual – entrepreneurs, bureaucrats, business lawyers, economists, engineers and industrial technicians. It is within the latter categories that he sees some potential for the development of an intelligentsia that is organic to the labour movement. In the modern world, he notes, 'technical education, closely bound to industrial labour . . . must form the basis of the new type of intellectual' (ibid.: 9). Only through understanding how industry works technically and administratively can the working class hope to wrest control from the bourgeoisie. While Gramsci describes this in terms of factory production, it would apply equally to other areas of political and economic life – to banking and finance, retail, the law and government.

It is insufficient, however, for organic intellectuals to *only* have technical knowledge. They must be willing to participate in the struggle for hegemony, to be 'directive' as well as 'specialized'. To achieve this, the organic intellectual must be able to elaborate their specialist knowledge into political knowledge. Whereas previous intellectuals relied on their sophistication and eloquence, the organic intellectual must actively participate in practical life, 'as constructor, organizer, "permanent persuader" and not just a simple orator' (ibid.: 10). This is certainly not to entirely reject older forms of knowledge. As Stuart Hall puts it, 'it is the job of the organic intellectual to know *more* than the traditional intellectuals do: really know, not just pretend to know . . . to know deeply and profoundly' (Hall 1996: 268).

For Gramsci, the typical organic intellectual of the proletariat is therefore likely to be someone who is technically trained and also a trade unionist or party activist – a figure who clearly owes much to his formative experience with the Turinese factory council movement. We might wish to extend this notion of the organic subordinate intellectual to new social movements and to issues of media representation, for it would be hard to imagine a contemporary organic intellectual who did not make use of media in their role as permanent persuaders. Certainly, some contemporary forms of subordination grant a very prominent role to activist-intellectuals' uses of the Internet. Downey and Fenton (2003) provide a review of these 'resource-poor' but technology-rich activists. They note that diverse campaigns, including the Mexican Zapatistas, the second Intifada in Israel/ Palestine and opposition to multinational food corporations, have adopted a common strategy of 'offline protest and online counter-publicity'. Within these movements, web intellectuals target the general public and the more established media sphere simultaneously. The fact that such persuasion is relatively non-hierarchical and diffuse would suggest a high level of overlap with Gramsci's ideal organic intellectual.

Gramsci's analysis of the intelligentsia is not simply a theory of revolutionary action but also an account of how authority has been exercised by dominant social groups. Gramsci observes that within modern capitalist society, the category of intellectuals has 'undergone an unprecedented expansion' (Gramsci 1971: 13). He is referring to the expanded stratum of bureaucrats, who seem to be autonomous of production even while they act in the interests of capitalism. Since his period, however, the numbers of 'intellectual' functions within both production and the state have massively increased, and more and more strata have emerged between the 'highest' and 'lowest' level of intellectual. To develop the idea of contemporary organic intellectuals concretely, we need to look elsewhere to understand how an emergent class creates together with itself 'an awareness of its function in the economic, social and political fields'.

The most influential commentator on these changes is Pierre Bourdieu, whose *Distinction* (1984) considers the emergence of new class fractions since the 1960s, and the ways in which taste comes to police the boundaries between classes and class fractions. Like Gramsci, Bourdieu argues that modern society generates new areas of production, which are accompanied by their own intellectuals. Perhaps the most productive of these is a new class stratum, the new petite bourgeoisie, or new lower middle class. Bourdieu argues that this group may be characterized as 'the new intellectuals', since its working role involves marking out new fields of knowledge and bodies of expertise. It provides bridges between the culture of the popular classes and the 'high' culture of the upper classes, and between work and leisure. The new petite bourgeoisie, he notes, thrive 'in all the occupations involving presentation and representation (sales, marketing, advertising, public relations, fashion, decoration and so forth) and in all the institutions providing symbolic goods and services' (Bourdieu 1984: 359)

This, therefore, is the class fraction most clearly organic to modern capitalism with its new forms of production and its 'knowledge economy'. But it is also a particularly valued class fraction in terms of its consumption choices, a subject on which Gramsci has very little to say. To use the idea of the organic intellectual in modern societies, we would therefore have to acknowledge that consumption is part of the intellectual's role. Commenting on this, Sean Nixon (1997) has noted that the new intelligentsia's identity gives great prominence to questions of pleasure, individualism and experimentation, values which circulate simultaneously as key *social* norms. It is, as Gramsci remarks, an 'integral conception of the world' in which the organic intellectual embodies the meanings and aspirations of the broader society.

We can make a series of further points about this new organic intelligentsia. First, it can be thought of spatially. The new petite bourgeoisie is concentrated in metropolitan centres, thereby rendering other places provincial or marginal – though this is likely to provoke the formation of a counter-hegemonic regional intelligentsia. Second, the new petite bourgeoisie is a group that, as well as being closely involved in representation, is itself extensively represented, and this representation becomes part of the struggle for hegemony. Throughout the 1980s, for example, images of the 'yuppie' circulated as a largely negative focus for various cultural, economic and political obsessions. Third, we should remember that these are intermediate strata rather than a new dominant class (which, for Bourdieu, is the more consolidated 'new bourgeoisie') and are therefore subalterns within the bloc and not necessarily its beneficiaries. Their function is analogous to that of civil society – providing a trench system that sustains capitalism through its complexity and interlocking levels. Finally, this group actively seeks engagement with 'the people' rather than adopting a disinterested pose. As Chaney (2002), Moores (2000) and Hollows (2003) have noted, using the examples of politicians, popular broadcasters and TV chefs respectively, new organic intellectuals are likely to adopt more informal styles of dress and diction than traditional authorities, and to articulate their own values to popular and often 'private' projects. While this may be no more than disingenuous populism, it also holds out the hegemonic promise that these intellectuals will themselves be reshaped by having to couch their appeal in popular terms. Engagement with the everyday is not a feature of intellectual life as it is conventionally understood, and it is to this that we now turn.

TRADITIONAL INTELLECTUALS

The opposite of the organic intellectual is, for Gramsci, the traditional thinker, and if one way of thinking about the former is as someone engaged with the messy complexity of social life, the traditional intelligentsia are characterized by their apparent withdrawal from such matters. In the *Prison Notebooks*, the stereotype of this figure is the 'man of letters, philosopher or artist', which may suggest that Gramsci sees such figures as dilettantes or parasites. Yet what these figures have in common is a belief that their specialism is disinterestedly autonomous of political considerations, and this would apply to knowledge professionals – teachers, medics, research scientists, economists, legal experts – just as much as it would apply to more obviously 'cultural' intellectuals.

One reason why we should not confuse the traditional intelligentsia with intellectual laziness or outmoded modes of thought is Gramsci's respect for the process of learning as a form of work. As we noted earlier, he resists the idea that working and thinking are separate phenomena, and describes the acquisition of knowledge as a 'job', an 'apprenticeship', a training involving muscles and nerves which anyone can achieve with sufficient labour. If people do not recognize education as a form of work, they will wrongly perceive it as a 'gift' or 'trick'. This reproduces social inequality, since learning appears to be the natural property of an elite. It is for this reason that Gramsci opposed the school reforms carried out by the Fascists, which advocated greater vocationalism. While acknowledging that vocational schools would allow lower-class children to 'improve themselves' through skills training, Gramsci argues that the rejection of rigorous, traditional education would 'crystallize' children in their lowly status. This is because they would be denied the intellectual tools needed to achieve educational parity with their social superiors. The opposition between vocational and traditional education remains very much a live debate, and you might consider the balance of the two in your own intellectual formation and judge whether Gramsci's position (which might now be considered elitist) continues to have any value.

It is precisely because older ideas continue to be useful that Gramsci sees one of the most urgent tasks facing any emergent political group as being the assimilation of the traditional intellectuals. Again, we need to think of this in the reflexive fashion that Gramsci's notion of hegemony encourages – a group cannot simply allow an existing intelligentsia to provide its intellectual leadership, because if it does it will be transformed. This might help explain, for example, how national liberation movements in the developing world have been reshaped into religious movements, or how socialist politics have been transformed by nationalism. Instead, an emergent group must develop its own organic intellectuals to a sufficient level whereby they can exercise hegemony over some or all of the traditional intelligentsia. Gramsci gives an example of this in the development of English society in the eighteenth and nineteenth centuries. In this period, he says, industrial capitalism replaced the landowning aristocracy as the ruling economic power in England. However, the industrial bourgeoisie ruled through proxy, with the aristocracy continuing to form the government and to provide cultural leadership. The style of the aristocracy was thus preserved while its economic power waned. So while England was rapidly being transformed into the world's most urban and industrial nation, its dominant image was reassuringly continuous – a land of rolling hills, country estates and contentedly fixed class status. This image served the industrial bourgeoisie through disguising its rule, though it has been argued that it too became seduced by the image and abandoned its 'industrial spirit' in favour of a nostalgic ruralism (Wiener 1981).

Gramsci presents the English aristocracy as gracefully acquiescing to its assimilation, but it is more common for a traditional intelligentsia to resist being incorporated into an emergent hegemony. This is because in the course of its development it has come to misrecognize itself as being outside political and everyday affairs. The material conditions of intellectual life might give some justification to this misconception. Gramsci's historical analysis of the Catholic Church, or indeed a roll-call of the faculty of any modern university, would suggest that intellectuals have a high degree of international mobility, or 'cosmopolitanism', and are therefore somewhat abstracted from local concerns. Equally, the intelligentsia has come to see itself as classless, a 'priesthood or caste' that is 'autonomous and independent of the dominant social group', despite the valuable ideological and administrative functions it performs on behalf of that group.

The key intellectual of this kind was, for Gramsci, Benedetto Croce. Although he had served as minister of education in the Fascist government, Croce came to oppose Mussolini, partly on the grounds that it was the responsibility of intellectuals to separate scholarship from politics. When a *Manifesto of Fascist Intellectuals* was produced, Croce claimed that politics and learning should not be mixed (Sassoon 1999: 19). Yet this pose of disinterestedness was, for Gramsci, a political action, since its role was to defend the bourgeois-liberal state in the face of fascism and communism. While Croce, he writes, may feel himself closely linked to the timeless philosophy of Aristotle and Plato, 'he does not conceal . . . his links with [the industrialists] Agnelli and Benni, and it is precisely here that one can discern the most significant character of Croce's philosophy' (Gramsci 1971: 8).

There are two ways, therefore, in which we might unpick Gramsci's binary opposition between organic and traditional intellectuals. On the one hand, traditional intellectuals were once organic to a class in its ascendancy, but now appear to be autonomous of that class, and may – in the case of dissident intellectuals and artistic avant-gardes – be critical of it, or embarrassing to it. Yet this autonomy might be functional to capitalism by offering a 'transcendent' alternative to reality. To turn to the eternal truths of religion, art or philosophy is also to turn away from more pressing problems of political responsibility (Eagleton 1991).

Second, the traditional intelligentsia may, like Croce, be forced into *becoming* organic to a class or cause if conditions threaten its autonomy. As new, contingent situations appear, intellectuals are forced into becoming organizers and persuaders. You could judge the extent of this oscillation between the poles of 'traditional' and 'organic' intellectual function by looking at the actions of religious leaders, Gramsci's paradigm of the traditional intelligentsia. Within normative periods, their intellectual activity is likely to be rather abstract and arcane. But over issues such as the ordination of women, gays and lesbians, the availability of contraception and abortion, questions of embryo research and the pursuit of war, religious intellectuals are cast in an organic role – forming alliances, organizing the media, seeking popular legitimation. The same would be true, with different foci, for scientists. From inward-looking issues, their skills are retrained towards the arena of popular consciousness and it is to that subject that we now turn.

INTELLECTUALS, POPULAR CULTURE AND COMMON SENSE

We saw earlier that Lenin's theory of the revolutionary vanguard argued for the imposition of socialist consciousness on the people of Russia. Superior wisdom is therefore transmitted downwards to the labouring classes. For Gramsci, however, the process of education is better conceived as a dialogue between intellectuals and 'the people'. 'Every leap forwards . . . of the intellectual stratum', he argues, 'is tied to an analogous movement on the part of the mass of the "simple"' (Sassoon 1999: 35). Intellectual guidance is sterile and pedantic unless it is embedded in the concerns and 'worldview' of the popular classes. 'The popular element', he writes, '"feels" but does not always know or understand; the intellectual element "knows" but does not always understand and in particular does not always feel' (Gramsci 1971: 418). Intellectuals must therefore learn how to feel, how to belong and how to become impassioned. Only then can they understand the aspirations of the people, represent them to those above, and elaborate 'a superior [more fully theorized] conception of the world' to those below. To make this 'sentimental connection' with the people-nation, intellectuals must be prepared to enter into, understand and use their culture. Only when 'feeling-passion' is made into understanding 'can there take place an exchange of individual elements between the rulers and ruled, leaders and led, and can the shared life be realized' (ibid.).

One of the characteristics of Italian intellectual life for Gramsci was that the intelligentsia were unprepared for this kind of engagement. Their interest in culture took the form of a preference for 'high' over popular culture, and they failed to produce any Italian tradition of popular literature. Thus representations 'of ways of thinking, "signs of the times" or changes occurring in people's behaviour are nowhere to be found' within the reading of these traditional intellectuals (Gramsci 1985: 274). Not only do these intellectuals therefore possess no understanding of the people's 'common sense' (beyond a feeling that it is inferior to their own conception of the world), but they are also prevented from elaborating its stock of 'good sense' into a progressive, cross-class project under their leadership.

Clearly, this situation has fundamentally changed in Italy and elsewhere. There has been a massive expansion in the number and type of intellectuals who produce, distribute and interpret popular culture. But conflict between more 'traditional' and more 'organic' responses to this material continues to be a prominent cultural motif. Moreover, it is clear that class society is not the only producer of 'dominant' ideas. What are the dominant ideas of gender, race and sexuality, and who are its intellectuals?

One piece of analysis that attempts to map this process of intervention, without reducing all issues to a question of class, is Andrew Ross's study of American intellectuals, *No Respect* (1989). I outline his work on 'The Pleasures of Pornography' since it makes two points strongly: first that we need to see intellectuals as a complex social group constantly shifting between positions of engagement and disengagement, and second that the pleasures of popular culture continue to be a problem for the intelligentsia. Pornography might seem an odd place to begin thinking about the politics of the people, but Ross notes that a hegemonic project that has nothing to say about fantasy and bodily gratification is failing to engage with a major component of common sense, and with a thriving sector of the culture industry. Picking up on the emergence of hardcore porn directed by women, he argues that this is the latest phase in the legitimization of pornography, a bid for respectability in which intellectuals have taken a particularly prominent role as both advocates and opponents.

Ross splits this process into two broad periods. In the first phase, discussion of pornography explored the boundaries of elite and popular taste. So, for example, the soft-core imagery of women in the upmarket *Playboy* was accompanied by writing produced by the literary intelligentsia that typically defended middle-class men's right to recreational sex and pornography as a form of art. Another stratum of pornographer-intellectuals rejected this traditionalist elitism in favour of seeing porn as a democratic medium giving access to authentic popular desires. From the late 1970s further strata joined the debate: intellectuals trying to separate pornography from erotica, or seeing it as a mode of avant-garde 'transgression', and sex workers who had become film directors or moral commentators. The intellectual field as constructed by these figures was therefore much more complex than a simple polarity of organic and traditional intellectuals. All the groups involved fulfilled some organic function to a particular group. *Playboy*'s advocacy of sex-as-fun, for example, was clearly tied into the emergence of a new middle class, while the debate about erotica was closely linked to 'second wave' feminism. But many of the terms in which the debate was carried out involved 'traditional' levels of abstraction and the assumption of cultural authority and good taste on the part of intellectuals.

Ross argues that the fundamental terms of this debate shifted in the 1980s as a consequence of the appearance of a group of vanguardist anti-porn feminist intellectuals, whose most prominent voices were Andrea Dworkin (1946–2005) and Catharine Mackinnon (1946–). This movement proposed that normative heterosexuality, represented through porn, was a unified vehicle for men to commit violence against women. Its utopian solution was to detach women totally from the 'contaminated culture of ordinary people' and to produce 'correct' representations, fantasies and sexual practices. This intellectual group proved successful in constructing a consistent ideology around porn at a time when the unity of the women's movement was being challenged. It therefore offered the leadership needed to give the movement renewed coherence. Ross points out, however, that in two ways this settlement was unsatisfactory. First, it relied on traditional views of media effects, which analysed culture in terms of 'mass manipulation, systematic domination and victimization' (Ross 1989: 177). Second, by isolating porn as the '*essential* issue of radical feminist attention' (ibid.: 187) and seeing it solely in terms of violence against women, antiporn feminists constructed a limited hegemonic project which could only address one constituency. It could not, for example, address the desires of sexual minorities such as gay men, nor could it deal with heterosexual women's appetite for explicit material, to which they had historically been denied access. Unable to resolve this limitation ideologically, antiporn feminists forced a 'coercive' solution to the impasse in the form of an alliance with non-feminist moralists demanding a greater degree of state censorship of sexually explicit material.

In the search for a more expansive response to these issues, Ross therefore notes the emergence of an 'anti-antiporn' movement of feminist intellectuals who aim to construct a broader constituency of people interested in representations of sexuality and thus resist vanguardism within the women's movement. However, here again the question of 'organic to whom?' appears, since this stratum has to negotiate pornography's status as a business and may thereby become the unwitting agents of a new phase in consumer capitalism. Writing in 1989, Ross stresses the way in which porn was central to the new consumer markets based around cable television and the VCR, but a similar analysis today would have to note the complex ways in which porn is bound up with the Internet, the information economy and the intellectuals who produce and mediate those phenomena. Moreover, Gramsci's identification of common sense as a disablingly alien form of thought for intellectuals is paramount. Ross claims that without truly understanding porn (without its 'feeling-passion'), intellectuals cannot hope to reconstruct the terrain of the popular since they will simply reproduce the critical distance of the traditional intelligentsia. What is at stake in the study of porn, he notes, 'is a cultural politics which seeks to *learn from* the forms and discourses of popular pleasure, rather than adopting or supporting a legislative and instructional posture' (ibid.: 207). If this leaves the question of how one could therefore criticize porn unanswered, then this, for Ross, is the price of complexity.

SUMMARY

This chapter has focused on Gramsci's distinction between traditional and organic intellectuals. It has argued that although these terms usefully draw attention to particular areas of cultural production and negotiation, it is impossible to think of them as entirely discrete phenomena. Instead, 'traditional' and 'organic' are porous to each other and force us to pay close attention to the production of knowledge in any period and its shifting links with social groups. The chapter has emphasized that the sheer diversity of ideas in circulation in any era indicates problems with the notion that the ruling bloc's ideas are 'epochal'. Using the example of pornography, we have seen that popular culture and common sense continue to mark out major fault-lines between different groups of intellectuals. The intensity, extent and duration of these differences indicate a crisis in sexual relations, and it is to the issue of crisis that we now turn.

7

CRISIS

So far we have concentrated on hegemony as a project that involves the formation of moral and intellectual consensus, under the leadership of a particular social group. However, Gramsci draws a distinction between this 'moment of consent' and a 'moment of force' in which consensus dissolves into dissensus. The recourse to coercive and authoritarian means of enforcing a group's rule is evidence that it has failed in its attempt to construct an expansive hegemony. By taking this action, the hegemonic group or class severely compromises its credibility, and must therefore work harder than ever to shore up its rule through whatever ideological, economic, political and legal resources it has at its disposal. This is a particularly urgent task since opposition forces are likely to seize upon this lack of consent in order to construct their own counter-hegemony and fill the consensual vacuum. We can therefore to some extent unpick Gramsci's opposition between the moments of consent and force, since the latter is likely to be a period of more intensive 'consensualization', even if consent itself is withheld.

To this period of heightened hegemonic activity, Gramsci gives the name *crisis*. Capitalism, he argues, is riven by deep and incurable problems which he calls its 'organic' crisis. This can be distinguished from more immediate and temporary conjunctural crises that can be settled one way or another, and which form the ground for political and cultural mobilization. A state of crisis, he argues, throws up atypical phenomena, such as charismatic and dangerous 'men of destiny'. Speaking over the heads of civil society, these 'Caesars' make direct appeals to 'the people'. But though they may be able to construct a temporary settlement of the crisis, their resolutions cannot be other than temporary ones, since fundamental problems are being suppressed. Mussolini was such a figure and the Fascists' seizure of power was, for Gramsci, a 'revolution/restoration', 'revolution without revolution' or *passive revolution*, which could not touch the essentials of class power. The history of post-Risorgimento Italy was, for Gramsci, a parade of such passive revolutions, in which the leaders of oppositional forces were repeatedly transformed into agents of the dominant social group, while the great mass of people remained without political representation.

This chapter therefore considers these issues – organic and conjunctural crisis, Caesarism and passive revolution – in greater theoretical depth. It illustrates them through analysis of a specific historical moment of crisis: the drift towards coercive solutions and the development of an 'exceptional state' in postwar Britain. We shall pay particular attention to one of the key texts in the Gramscian tradition: Stuart Hall, Chas Critcher, Tony Jefferson, John Clarke and Brian Roberts's *Policing the Crisis* (1978). This major work points to the ways that 'crisis' manifests itself in a moral panic around the criminal behaviour of young black men, which appears to be independent of the crisis of capitalism. The chapter then looks at this moment through the lens of fictional representation, seeing how authoritarian solutions are negotiated within popular culture.

ORGANIC CRISIS

As we have seen, Gramsci characterizes civil society as a 'powerful system of fortresses and earthworks'. The ruling social group has at its disposal a formidable array of institutions and techniques for maintaining its authority, and the task of disentangling these interlinked defences is a daunting one for counter-hegemonic forces. Nonetheless, there will come a time in the life of the ruling group when it is either unable to satisfy the aspirations of its subalterns, or is overtaken by some contingent event. As Gramsci puts it:

> In every country the process is different, although the content is the same. And the content is the crisis of the ruling class's hegemony, which occurs either because the ruling class has failed in some major political undertaking for which it has requested, or forcibly extracted, the consent of the broad masses (war, for example), or because huge masses . . . have

> passed suddenly from a state of political passivity to a certain activity, and put forward demands which taken together, albeit not organically formulated, add up to a revolution. A 'crisis of authority' is spoken of: this is precisely the crisis of hegemony, or general crisis of the State.
>
> (Gramsci 1971: 210)

Gramsci is thinking here about the ways in which political parties represent particular class interests, though we may extend his argument to think about any representative body that organizes a large constituency of people (religions, community leaders, trade unions, scientists, etc.). In all of these cases, the represented may reject their leadership. This 'conjunctural' crisis differs from an organic crisis since it may be rectified, within limits, by the ruling group. Indeed, Gramsci observes that the ruling class is more likely than its opponents to regain control in a situation of crisis since it has trained 'cadres' of potential leaders waiting in the wings. The ruling class may be weakened through the need to make sacrifices but it is still able to dispense with its adversaries and recover its power.

Even if this is a common outcome, however, Gramsci does not claim it is the inevitable outcome. It may be that the equilibrium of forces is such that the ruling class cannot impose its will. Or it may succeed in reinstating its authority but at the price of a devastating loss of ideological credibility. Although the coercive apparatuses of the state are never entirely absent within democracies (think of the prominence of courts, military pageantry, the police and so on) it is, as Terry Eagleton remarks, 'preferable on the whole for power to remain conveniently invisible, disseminated throughout the texture of social life and "naturalized" as custom, habit, spontaneous practice' (Eagleton 1991: 116). By shifting its mode of direction towards coercion, the state shows that, first, its authority is always finally dependent upon armed force rather than popular consent, and second that it is not a neutral arbiter between social groups, but instead a highly interested party. As an added complication, it may be the case that various groups within the state's coercive arms have different objectives to the ruling class. These objectives are only animated during moments of crisis, but once unleashed come to exist beyond the control of democratic rulers. The 'rogue' behaviour of the police and security forces at various times indicates the potential for such violent solutions.

Finally, while the preceding discussion might indicate that the crisis is always a period of 'hot' conflict (and Gramsci's persistent resort to military metaphors points the reader in that direction), it is equally sustainable to theorize it as a crisis of values that are played out within popular culture. At one point in the *Prison Notebooks*, Gramsci refers to the crisis as a kind of ailment, accompanied by 'morbid symptoms' and 'depression' (Gramsci 1971: 275). Popular culture provides a means of mapping this morbidity. We therefore need to be particularly attentive to those patterns within representation where a 'problem' is delineated and a repressive textual resolution to the problem articulated. In some cases these representations may cohere with the coercive activities of the state. For example, fictional and factual coverage of the 'War On Drugs' accompanies and to some extent authorizes the activities of police forces. In other cases, however, texts may indicate a state of crisis that is independent of the state. Feminist scholars have identified a spate of 'backlash' movies (*Fatal Attraction*, 1987; *Single White Female*, 1992; *The Hand that Rocks the Cradle*, 1992) in which independent female characters are depicted as psychotic and killed off in the final reel. This symbolic violence, they argue, is implicated in an attempted reassertion of masculine authority in the face of a general crisis of patriarchy (see Hollows 2002). Textual solutions, however, are typically more ambivalent than state coercion, and we consider such attempts to symbolically manage crisis later in the chapter.

PASSIVE REVOLUTION

Whether through coercive or symbolic means, Gramsci proposes that the crisis can be resolved in favour of a ruling social group. However, this resolution is unlikely to be permanent or satisfactory. One of Gramsci's axioms, drawn from Marx, is that a 'social formation' (a class or class fraction) cannot disappear while its productive forces 'still find room for further forward movement' (Sassoon 1999: 16). By reasserting its authority (even in modified form) and failing to draw subordinates such as the working class into its hegemony, a declining ruling class impedes the development of these productive forces, a failure to which Gramsci gives the name 'passive revolution'.

For Gramsci, the Risorgimento was the key example of a passive revolution. During and after Unification, the Italian bourgeoisie had the opportunity to construct a genuine national-popular in which they would lead the popular classes, while also responding to their aspirations. Instead, they constructed a minority political class based on the Moderate Party, which gradually absorbed and transformed the leadership of the radical Action Party. This bourgeois elite, writes Gramsci, was 'characterised by its aversion to any intervention of the popular masses in state life, to any organic reform which would substitute a "hegemony" for its crude, dictatorial "dominance"' (Gramsci 1971: 58n.). Without a truly popular mandate for its rule, the Italian bourgeoisie was therefore susceptible to a series of crises, culminating in the rise of fascism. Gramsci sees a fundamental connection between the period of *trasformismo* and Mussolini's rise to power, since both are 'revolutions from above' rather than hegemonic projects. In both the state is forced into a high level of intervention, which does not rely on the active participation and consent of the people.

It would thus be quite possible to have a socialist or social-democratic passive revolution, as Gramsci indicates when he points to Franklin D. Roosevelt's New Deal as another manifestation of the phenomenon. Lingering around this is a suspicion of the state as a vehicle for coercion. We might wish to think more reflexively about the connections between the people and the state today. Given the concerted neo-liberal assault that has taken place on western welfare states over the past three decades, it seems questionable to represent the state as a vehicle for the interests of the ruling class. Nonetheless, we should take seriously Gramsci's proposition that radical change without democratic participation simply reproduces authoritarian and patronizing assumptions about the relationship between leaders and led.

CAESARISM

During periods of passive revolution, the ruling class exercises its authority. However, Gramsci postulates another situation, in which the two 'fundamental' classes in a historical period (the aristocracy and the bourgeoisie, or the bourgeoisie and the proletariat) are so balanced that neither class can hegemonize or dominate the other. He calls this situation a 'static equilibrium' or 'interregnum', arguing that an organic crisis 'consists precisely in the fact that the old is dying and the new cannot be born; in this interregnum a great variety of morbid symptoms appear' (Gramsci 1971: 275). One such morbid symptom is the charismatic 'man of destiny', who offers the leadership necessary to overcome the impasse and construct a new settlement based on the force of their personality. While sometimes using the word 'Bonapartism' to describe this situation (see box), Gramsci more commonly uses the term 'Caesarism', after the Roman autocrat Julius Caesar. In adopting this term, he is mindful of Mussolini's claims to be a 'new Caesar'.

BONAPARTISM

The term Bonapartism is drawn from Marx's pamphlet *The Eighteenth Brumaire of Louis Bonaparte* (1852) in which he explains the *coup d'état* that brought Emperor Napoleon III to power in 1851. For Marx, France was unstable after 1815 because the bourgeoisie, divided by economic and political factionalism, could not exert its authority as a class. Instead the state came to hold a dangerous degree of autonomy, particularly in the stalemate that followed the revolution of 1848. Napoleon was an answer to this crisis, and although he appeared to rule on behalf of a dying class, the conservative peasantry, his imposition of order actually worked in the long-term interest of the bourgeoisie by preventing proletarian revolution. The class struggle in France thus 'created circumstances and relationships that made it possible for a grotesque mediocrity to play a hero's part'.

More generally, the term Bonapartism refers to a situation in which the army or police and the state bureaucracy intervene to re-establish order during a period of static equilibrium. It thus provides a way of thinking about later developments such as the rule of military juntas, Stalinism and Nazism. Gramsci's Caesarism is a broader term, since it also covers tendencies within democracies.

It is the sheer complexity of civil society that paradoxically makes such Caesarist interventions feasible. Having slowly built up the apparent autonomy of civil society, the ruling social group is unable to quickly mobilize it in moments of static equilibrium. Charismatic figures therefore present themselves as being able to 'get the job done' without the time-consuming need to win over the institutions of civil society. Caesarist figures are thus likely to be populist leaders who make direct, personal appeals to the people. Such populism should not be confused with democracy, since it does not involve building up the infrastructure through which people could genuinely participate in decision-making. As a consequence, Gramsci argues that in the modern world, a Caesarist solution does not demand a Caesar, since a political party can fulfil the same functions of spouting populist slogans while maintaining a monopoly over the mechanisms of power. It so happens, however, that many Caesarist episodes *do* involve 'heroic' or 'maverick' individuals. These figures do not need to be warlike in the manner of the men whom Gramsci lists as Caesars. Indeed, a modern Caesar was someone who presented herself as anti-authoritarian and peace-loving. Both in life, but much more significantly in her death, Diana, Princess of Wales was made to speak on behalf of a variety of populist issues. Described as a 'Queen of Hearts' and 'People's Princess', Diana provided a magical resolution to all kinds of social ills (Britain's arms trade, the marginal position of social minorities, and the anachronism of the monarchy). The fact that no democratic mechanisms were built up through which these things might be tackled is indicative of its Caesarism.

Perhaps surprisingly, Gramsci does not always see Caesarism as being reactionary. To understand this apparent inconsistency, we might remember his indebtedness to Machiavelli, particularly *The Prince*'s contention that the soldier-scholar can provide the centre of a 'national-popular'. Caesarism may therefore take a 'progressive' form when the intervention of the 'great personality' allows emergent social forces to triumph, and a conversely 'reactionary' form when conservative forces are victorious (Gramsci 1971: 219). In both cases, however, these victories are liable to be tempered by compromises and limitations.

Elsewhere, however, Gramsci is rather less persuaded that men of destiny can be anything other than reactionary. His analysis of military elites (1971: 211–17) makes the point that their class origin precludes them from having certain aptitudes (such as organizing an economy), and that they have particular institutional loyalties that operate outside the terms of democratic governments. He therefore warns against aping the methods of these elites, 'for one will fall into easy ambushes'. One such ambush lies in wait for those who think that violent action is of equivalent utility to the building up of democratic-popular institutions within civil society. Since Gramsci's philosophy is predicated on the need to fight a long-term 'war of position' rather than a dramatic 'war of manoeuvre', Caesarist solutions will simply promote further crises. As Paul Buchanan (2000) has noted, the collapse of dictatorial and colonial regimes around the world over the past 30 years has not inevitably led to the establishment of democratic politics in their place. Instead authoritarianism has shown itself to be remarkably persistent and self-perpetuating. Examples drawn from eastern Europe, southern Africa and Latin America 'suggest the disproportionate strength personalities have in constructing the fortunes of post-authoritarian societies as well as the tendency towards alternative forms of authoritarian leadership' (Buchanan 2000: 115). We examine a 'charismatic' attempt to reconstruct a democratic society below.

POLICING THE CRISIS

In what follows, we work through the notions of crisis, passive revolution and Caesarism by way of a particular historical example, Hall *et al.*'s (1978) analysis of the 'mugging' panic of the early 1970s. *Policing the Crisis* attempts to capture the full range of 'political, juridical and ideological' forms in circulation in Britain between 1945 and the mid-1970s in order to show how consent became progressively exhausted in postwar British society, and was replaced by what they term the 'exceptional state'. The crisis of capitalism, they maintain, was managed through the adoption of increasingly authoritarian representations of, and solutions to, social problems which came to cohere around the 'alien' figure of the black mugger.

Policing the Crisis argues that Britain, between the end of the Second World War and the mid-1960s, appeared to be a consensual society, characterized by political stability, high levels of employment, rising incomes, a prolonged consumer boom and the implementation of a 'cradle-to-grave' welfare state. This settlement was accompanied by a series of party political discourses that identified Britain as a pragmatic and democratic society in which an upper-class 'Establishment' had been displaced by a cross-class meritocracy. In the first period identified by the authors, the uninterrupted years of Conservative rule between 1951 and 1963, the key term became 'affluence', the idea that Britain was moving from postwar austerity and rationing to a period of unprecedented material prosperity and 'classlessness'. During the succeeding Labour administration of 1963–66 the keyword was 'modernization', with the Labour Prime Minister, Harold Wilson, famously prophesying that a New Britain would be 'forged in the white heat of the technological revolution'.

If Britain was such a consensual society, then it is worth asking why such prominent political statements were necessary. The answer for Hall *et al.* is that Britain's postwar recovery was drastically incomplete. The loss of the British Empire, low levels of investment, high levels of inflation, and the privileged position of finance capitalism ensured that Britain was in a disadvantageous manufacturing position in relation to its rivals. At the same time, the assumed dissolution of class society turned out to have been overstated. Rising average wages disguised the maintenance of rigid class differences and the survival of pockets of severe deprivation in the UK.

These, then, were the 'major political undertakings' in which the ruling class was unsuccessful. 'Affluence' and 'modernization' were passive revolutions which failed to reconstruct the real relations between rulers and ruled into a more inclusive settlement. Inseparable from this failure was a crisis of values and authority. Hall *et al.* note that the first signs of moral crisis emerged in the 1950s, at the very moment of affluence. In particular, conservative anxieties about the new consumer society cohered around an image of 'lawless' and 'hedonistic' youth. At a very early stage, this youth problem became associated with questions of race, initially as a consequence of white youths attacking black immigrants, but later as blackness itself came to be seen as a problem. As the economic crisis deepened, the intensity of these moral fears increased. Moreover, the number of assumed threats to social order expanded to include organized crime, sexual 'permissiveness', student activism, and civil rights in Northern Ireland.

Hall *et al.* make a number of points about the mechanisms by which this 'subterranean' body of fairly incoherent anxieties were elaborated, above all in the news media, into a full-blown moral panic. They note that two strategies in particular cause an escalation in the response of both the state and the public to social order, so that the reaction becomes '*out of all proportion* to the actual threat offered' (ibid.: 16). The first of these they call 'convergence', in which parallels are drawn between quite discrete issues to imply a fundamental connection between them. The second is the crossing of 'thresholds', which automatically triggers progressively greater coercive responses. By 1968, the year they identify as critical, a number of perceived thresholds had been crossed – around permissiveness, legality and protestors' use of violence – all of which resulted in calls for 'something to be done'. These demands were met by a greater willingness to use the police and legal apparatus against transgressors. The key convergence of 1968 was between student revolts throughout western metropolises and the presence of black people in Britain.

It was a Caesarist intervention that most potently secured this convergence. On 20 April 1968 Enoch Powell delivered what became known as the 'Rivers of Blood' speech, predicting race war in Britain and accusing successive Conservative and Labour governments of betraying the 'respectable' white population. Hall *et al.* argue that Powell recognized that the postwar consensus had reached a static equilibrium, in which neither of the main political parties could generate forward movement. He therefore appealed over the head of the political process (his speech was timed to coincide with a Race Relations Bill) to a popular constituency that he claimed were unrepresented, offering himself as their voice. His choice of race as a focus for social and economic fragmentation, *Policing the Crisis* argues, was effective because it was a *direct* appeal to the everyday lives and disappointed ambitions of those 'respectable' working and lower-middle class people forced into living in the 'visibly declining parts of the post-imperial city' (ibid.: 244).

Powell did not, in fact, emerge as a credible leader of this constituency, but his intervention filled the vacuum left by the dying consensus, and it did so by shifting the centre of political debate towards authoritarianism. In the prelude to the 1970 General Election, and subsequently in office, the Conservative Party put forward authoritarian solutions to a host of public order issues, from trade union militancy, through immigration to petty vandalism. As *Policing the Crisis* observes, the Conservatives' law-and-order policies 'had the overwhelming single consequence of legitimating the recourse to the law, to constraint and statutory power, as the . . . only, effective means left of defending hegemony in conditions of severe crisis' (ibid.: 278). It was this moment that, for Hall *et al.*, Britain became an exceptional state (or more precisely it was an 'exceptional moment' in the 'normal' operations of a capitalist state experiencing long-term crisis). Within the exceptional state, there is a tendency to see all threats to social order as a transgression of the highest threshold, that of violence.

The crisis therefore germinated in a number of areas: in Britain's long-term economic decline; in politicians' failure to represent a 'silent majority' of disaffected Britons; in the persistent recourse to race as a general explanation of social ills; in the British media's willingness to amplify the threat of crime; and in the authoritarian drift of the Conservative Party, civil society and the state. It was this coming-together of disparate elements that, for Hall *et al.*, made the conjunctural crisis of the 1972 mugging panic inevitable. All the essential 'conditions [of a moral panic]', they write, 'are met in full at the moment when the "mugging panic" precipitates' (ibid.: 306).

There are a number of important criticisms of *Policing the Crisis*. Its assumptions about the ways in which subordinate social groups take up the messages transmitted by leading groups are questionable. While Hall *et al.* posit the existence of an 'authoritarian consensus', they provide little evidence of this beyond the press's claims for such unity (see Barker 1992; Stabile 2001). Moreover, the book never quite shakes off the problem of how far race is determined by class. Nonetheless, we have seen how Gramsci's key terms for understanding a crisis can be put to use in the analysis of contemporary society. You may wish to use *Policing the Crisis* as a template for analysing contemporary moral panics (over, for example, guns, gangs, drugs and immigration), evaluating the usefulness of its understanding of crisis in a different epoch. We move on to see how such crises are differently managed within popular culture.

REPRESENTING THE CRISIS

In his cultural writings, Gramsci deals briefly with the ways in which popular fictions are caught up in the political crisis. As we have seen, he argued that most of Italy's popular literature came from elsewhere – particularly from France – since there was no native tradition of producing such narratives. But while Gramsci treats the production of popular literature as being a necessary condition of the establishment of a national-popular, he is briskly dismissive of the worldview of these fictions. The focus of this diatribe is Eugene Sue's serial novel *The Mysteries of Paris* (1842–43). The hero of this early thriller is one Prince Rodolphe, a figure who scours the Parisian underworld, dispensing justice to wrongdoers and rewarding the virtuous. Gramsci sees a clear relationship between the text's narrative drive and the behaviour of the Fascists. This, he writes, 'is the romantic setting in which the fascist mentality is formed' (Gramsci 1985: 346n.). Just as Mussolini imposed a Caesarist solution to the weakness of Italian social democracy, so Prince Rodolphe is a Caesarist figure who 'paralyses' the class struggle. *The Mysteries of Paris* and similar texts both produce and mimic fascism since they share its 'unbalanced imagination, quivering of heroic fury [and] psychological restlessness'. Like fascism, this adventure fiction is both nostalgic and committed to a violent reordering of society.

Gramsci therefore argues that romantic popular novels were an element in the cultural construction of fascism rather than its cultural output. However, like the news media mentioned in the previous section, fictional texts represent the crisis, mediating it through their generic conventions. I therefore want to look at some of the fictional output of the period covered by *Policing the Crisis*, which also deal with the law-and-order drift and the rise of the exceptional state. There is a high level of correspondence between some of the features of crisis identified by Gramsci (maverick figures, violent solutions, and police forces 'making other arrangements') and the content of these fictions. At the same time, however, Gramsci's assumption that popular fictions and authoritarian social groups speak with one voice is untenable. As a consequence of their need to address a specific public in terms of its own tastes, popular texts offer a more *ambivalent* interpretation of the crisis and its possible resolution.

It is certainly true that violence and law-and-order are prominent motifs within early 1970s cultural production. In the cinema, for example, films such as *Get Carter*, *Villain*, *The Offence*, *Straw Dogs* and *A Clockwork Orange* (all 1971) depicted Britain as violently fragmented and imposed a variety of coercive narrative solutions on those figures (underworld bosses, pornographers, youth gangs) held to be responsible for the anarchy. Yet despite this tendency towards authoritarian resolutions, there are grounds for seeing these texts as negotiations of the crisis rather than vehicles for the law-and-order drift. One reason for this is that two of these films, *Straw Dogs* and *A Clockwork Orange*, were themselves at the centre of moral panics. Film censorship in Britain has traditionally been carried out at arm's length through the quasi-autonomous British Board of Film Classification (BBFC). But when the BBFC appeared to renege on its gatekeeper role by passing *Straw Dogs* with minor cuts and *A Clockwork Orange* uncut, the Board itself became a focus for fears around permissiveness. The state, in alliance with conservative moral watchdogs, mobilized against both the films and the liberalism of the BBFC. Representation of these issues within news media served to amplify the assumed threat, linking the release of *A Clockwork Orange*, for example, with copycat violence.

Furthermore, these texts are typically ambivalent about the law-and-order drift. This ambiguous response to authoritarianism was also apparent in more mainstream texts. *The Sweeney*, for example, was a long-running television police drama which introduced a new level of grittiness and authenticity to the representation of law-and-order. But as Leon Hunt (1997, 1999) has shown, the pleasures of the programme, and more particularly its two cinematic spin-offs, were not necessarily those of the capitalist state imposing order on its adversaries. The real villain in the first film, he argues, is not an individual criminal but 'bad' capitalism (1999: 139). While the generic conventions of the police thriller mean that the protagonist, Regan (John Thaw) can do nothing about this general state of affairs, the film opens up a gap between the dominant class and the state forces that are, under normal conditions, its representatives. Similarly in the second film, Regan is tasked with stopping a gang of armed robbers who have adopted their own violent solutions to the problem of Britain's future. Hunt argues that these villains are represented in terms of a 'lurking fascism' (the logical conclusion of the authoritarian drift) at odds with Regan's 'underdog populism'. Such popular texts therefore negotiate the crisis of authority rather than reflecting coercive solutions to it.

The Sweeney's graphic violence was seen at the time as drawing on conventions of representing violence that had been established in America during the late 1960s. Just as mugging was interpreted as an 'Americanized' act of criminality (Hall *et al*. 1978: 3), so the new realism of British visual culture was assumed to be bound up with the pernicious influence of the United States. It is to Gramsci's thoughts on this issue, and its relationship with economic change, that we turn next.

SUMMARY

This chapter has looked at Gramsci's notion of crisis, seeing how he distinguishes between the organic crisis of capitalism and its short-term manifestations. It has argued that new expressions of cultural leadership appear during a time of crisis, some of which involve the establishment of authoritarian personality cults. Through an analysis of *Policing the Crisis* and the popular cultural production of the early 1970s, we have seen the increased level of hegemonic activity that takes place in a period of crisis. While the shift towards coercion indicates the arrival of 'iron times', it does not mean that the need to establish a consensus has ended. Indeed, the nature of coercion itself becomes the subject of dialogue, with state coercion having to construct a correspondence with authoritarian currents existing within popular culture and common sense.

8

AMERICANISM AND FORDISM

Although Gramsci makes some illuminating comments on the international trends of his time, there is little sustained analysis of the operations of hegemony outside Italy. The exception is his extensive discussion of Americanization in Europe. While a common observation about the American economy at various historical moments has been precisely its chaotic lack of regulation, Gramsci argues that Americanism and Fordism are the processes through which economic individualism and *laissez-faire* are transformed into a planned economy. It is thus possible to detach Americanism from America, since Fascist Italy, Soviet Russia and later Nazi Germany and the western democracies also experimented with economic planning. Equally, large parts of the United States were less subject to industrialization than Gramsci implies. However, for the most part Gramsci is indeed dealing with America as the home and symbol of a new phase of capitalist accumulation. He therefore writes within the tradition of European theorizations of American political economy established by Alexis de Tocqueville's *Democracy in America* (1835–40).

Fordism is named after the car manufacturer Henry Ford, who originated the first large-scale production line, while the 'scientific management' theorist Frederick Taylor (1856–1915) gave his name to *Taylorism*, a rationalized form of industrial production in which production was broken down into specific physical actions. Although these transformations were initially experienced in the production sector, their ramifications were felt in other arenas of social life. So, for example, the state had to provide the macro-economic conditions needed for this new form of mass production, while the private lives of workers were affected by new welfare rights and calls to participate in a 'consumer democracy' (Lee 1993: 82). These changes had consequences for subaltern and dominant groups since both were subjected to new processes of manipulation and rationalization. While the working class were disciplined into new ways of working, consuming and behaving, the 'parasites' of the old order became anachronisms within Fordist society. Gramsci asked whether these changes were sufficiently novel to justify describing them as forming a new historical 'epoch', or whether they were merely an intensification of processes already in existence. If the latter, then Americanism is another variation on the theme of passive revolution discussed in the previous chapter. Fordism, this argument posits, was a response to the world crisis triggered by the Wall Street Crash of 1929 and the subsequent Great Depression. One indication that Americanism was indeed a form of passive revolution was that, in Fascist Italy and elsewhere, Fordist practices were imposed on the economy 'from outside' (by legal and governmental means) rather than emerging organically from within the industrial 'base'. Finally, there are questions of Americanism as a cultural force, spreading distinctly modern attitudes throughout the world in forms as diverse as cinema, jazz and psychoanalysis – popular culture certainly, but posing problems for any existing or emerging national-popular.

The remainder of the chapter is therefore organized around these concerns. We move from a discussion of the fate of the 'parasitic' class under Americanism to consideration of the incorporation of working men and women within the Americanist-Fordist regime. We then look at responses to the Americanization of popular culture in Europe, before finally looking at Americanism's position within contemporary processes of globalization.

PARASITES AND PASSIVE SEDIMENTATIONS

The key to understanding America, for Gramsci, is its short history as a nation and its rapid industrial development. This meant that it never built up the many intermediate classes that existed in Europe, classes that fulfilled no significant role in the world of production and were therefore parasitic on the 'fundamental' classes who engage in or organize production. Although Gramsci groups all these intermediaries together, we might note that they fall into two categories. On the one hand are those 'passive sedimentations', which include the clergy, the civil service, military officers and the intelligentsia, that may have once fulfilled organic functions but which had fossilized into a large and burdensome salariat. More directly parasitic were the financial speculators and rural landlords who leased agricultural land to the peasantry in return for rents. While the cultivators of the land existed in a state of near-starvation, these figures lived in considerable luxury in the city.

Gramsci makes the point that the city itself becomes a parasite under these exploitative conditions. His example is Naples, the great city of the *Mezzogiorno*, though his analysis would hold true for many other European and colonial metropolises in the nineteenth century. Since the Southern landowners chose to live in Naples rather than on their estates, the economy of the city became devoted to satisfying their needs. Rather than Naples producing commodities for trade and an industrial workforce, it produced an army of servants, artisans and tradespeople who served the land-owning families. 'Where a horse shits', Gramsci observes, 'a hundred sparrows feed' (Gramsci 1971: 283). The cost of maintaining this unproductive servant class led to further extortion of the countryside as the rural poor were preyed upon by an intermediary class of bailiffs, land agents and mafias.

Gramsci was either unaware or unwilling to consider that these processes were also applicable to America, where sharecropping was common and where, particularly in the rural South, class coercion was compounded by racial oppression. Instead his analysis concentrates on the predominantly northern manufacturing centres of the United States. Here the virtual absence of the parasite stratum enabled industry to become established. Whereas a city like Naples was essentially inward-looking, the vision of Americanized industrial capitalism was outward, towards the production and distribution of new goods through which to capture popular consumer markets throughout the world. Fordist hegemony, he notes, 'is born in the factory and requires for its exercise only a minute quantity of professional and ideological intermediaries' (ibid.). The European parasite class therefore fears these developments and attempts to resist them, since they will 'sweep them away implacably'. As we shall see, this resistance takes place ideologically, as the intellectuals of the class attempt to drive a wedge between European 'high' culture and American popular culture. Yet if, for Gramsci, this dominant class stratum is ultimately doomed, what of the subordinate class under Americanism?

WORKERS, MORALITY AND PLEASURE

In one of his prison letters to his sister-in-law Tatiana, Gramsci records that his wife Giulia suffered a nervous breakdown from overwork. This, he says, is evidence of an increasing phenomenon, the importation of Fordist working practices and American management techniques even into Soviet Russia. Ford, he digresses:

> has a body of inspectors who supervise and regulate the private life of his employees: they superintend the foods, the beds, the cubic capacity of the rooms, the rest hours and even more intimate matters. Whoever does not conform is dismissed and loses his minimum salary of six dollars a day. Ford pays this minimum, but wants people who know how to work and who are always fit for work, in other words, who know how to coordinate their work with their way of life.
>
> (Gramsci 1979: 182)

Gramsci was hardly the first thinker to observe that industrialization imposed a new discipline on working people, based around their fitness to fulfil specific roles within factory production. Charles Dickens's *Hard Times* (1854) described factory workers being reduced to the status of 'hands' since their minds were not required by factory capitalism, while Marx and Engels's *Communist Manifesto* (1872) describes the worker as 'an appendage of the machine'. Nearer Gramsci's period, Upton Sinclair's *The Jungle* (1906) depicts the rigours of production line work in the Chicago abattoirs some years before the establishment of Ford's car plant. Taylorism and Fordism therefore merely represented an intensification of this deskilled and repetitive form of labour. As Gramsci repeatedly points out, Taylor claimed that factory work was so crude that it could be carried out by a trained gorilla. Yet while Gramsci concedes that automation will pitilessly eliminate part of the old working class, he warns against the pessimism that this vision of industrial humanity might induce. This is not, he says, 'the spiritual death of man'. For once the worker has adapted to the speed and nature of the task, without being eliminated, he or she will be able to carry it out automatically, leaving greater opportunities for thought – particularly the thought that workers are not trained apes, and that their work gives them no satisfaction. These thoughts are the basis of a revolutionary consciousness.

The two truly original features of Fordism for Gramsci are the priority it gives (at least in the short term) to higher wages and its concentration on the worker's leisure time. This is the context for Ford's enquiries into his workers' private lives – they represented an attempt to create a new kind of human being as well as a new kind of worker. This reconstruction took place on the terrain of moral, educational and health issues but it was not, for Gramsci, some humanist project of spiritual improvement. Instead, it had the aim of equipping workers psychologically and physically for the new methods of production. This was intended not only to maximize profit by improving output, but also to minimize the need to keep replacing workers, for the worker is, to the capitalist, 'a machine which cannot, without considerable loss, be taken to pieces too often and renewed with single new parts' (Gramsci 1971: 303). Since it would be too obviously a strategy of industrial control if these moral reforms were imposed upon the workers, Gramsci argues that the most durable 'puritanical' projects are those that emerge from either the apparently neutral arena of the state, or which are proposed by the workers themselves.

The specific examples that he gives of these reforms are the Volstead Act of 1920 (better known as Prohibition), and the reconstruction of sexual relations that took place during the period. Although there can be little doubt that America did enter a long period of consensus about these issues – even allowing for the repeal of the Volstead Act in 1933 – this may be as much about the deep roots of Christian morality within American life as the operations of the economic base. Indeed, Gramsci's argument here seems immune to the historical sensitivity that normally characterizes his analysis of cultural phenomena. While it is obvious that industrial managers will take a dim view of their employees' over-indulgence in sex and alcohol, it is by no means clear that working people are similarly inclined towards abstention – Ford's experiments, after all, were not entirely successful. Gramsci seems undecided whether these changes are therefore imposed upon the working class, or if they gel with an existing proletarian resentment towards upper-class decadence. He claims that workers did not mount any opposition to Prohibition, and that 'the corruption brought about by bootlegging and gangsterism was widespread amongst the upper classes' (ibid.: 299). Similarly, he presents a new openness about sex in interwar America as a bourgeois phenomenon. It is the upper classes, he claims, who treat women as objects of display, through beauty competitions, advertising, film and the theatre, while upper-class women demonstrate a morbid form of sexual independence in which they contract and leave marriages at will (ibid.: 306).

All this is somewhat contradictory. Elsewhere Gramsci shows himself sympathetic to feminism, arguing that women must attain genuine independence in relation to men, both in terms of work and in sexual relations (1979: 294). Moreover, his letters take an unmoralizing attitude towards many manifestations of sexuality, including interracial marriage (ibid.: 218), pre-marital sex and casual divorce (ibid.: 199). What is perhaps crucial about these phenomena is that he associates them with the country-side and therefore the pre-modern world. When dealing with contemporary reality, Gramsci commonly reverts to a kind of 'left puritanism' in which industrial workers are assumed to have higher standards of morality than either the peasantry or the upper classes. In some ways this is an *intellectual* response at odds with Gramsci's personal liberalism. In the same letter that begins this section, he presents his ambivalence over moral issues as a political act. European intellectuals, he claims, oppose the Fordist 'mechanization' of private life through a posture of Bohemianism. 'We're absurdly romantic', he writes, 'and in our efforts not to be bourgeois, we fall into Bohemianism which is in fact the most typical form of bourgeois behaviour' (ibid.: 182). Yet it is equally romantic to depict the working class as repositories of moral rectitude. While the theatre may have continued to be middle class, and divorce a rarity within European societies, beauty pageants and the sexual imagery of the cinema were popular pleasures, enjoyed by working-class men and women.

The problems and contradictions that Gramsci faced in working through Fordism's reconstruction of the individual suggest two related problems in his work – the character of the petite bourgeoisie and the theorization of popular pleasure. Puritanism, high wages and workplace discipline cannot entirely explain Fordism's triumph. It is surely also the case that it success-fully engaged in the production of pleasure, particularly the pleasures of consumption (after all, who were driving Ford's cars? And to do what?). By never developing a theory of consumption, whether of goods or of Fordist cultural forms such as cinema, it can be argued that Gramsci's work is trapped in precisely the position of intellectual externality that he elsewhere condemns.

Equally, we need to produce a more nuanced understanding of class culture than Gramsci allows for. Although he points out that many inter-mediate strata exist between the proletariat and the factory owners, and that hegemony involves the formation of cross-class alliances, he tends to caricature the lower-middle class as an essentially reactionary class fraction that provided a recruiting ground for fascism. As a consequence, beyond some thoughts on Sinclair Lewis's novel *Babbitt* (1922), he ignores the petite bourgeoisie under Fordism. Yet it may be that it was in this fraction that

Fordism's most successful moral reconstructions of the individual took place. At a number of junctures in *The Prison Notebooks*, Gramsci makes the point that one feature of Americanism is the diffusion of Freudian ideas about individual psychology. He does not elaborate on this in class terms. Yet as Sue Currell (2006) has shown, it was within the realms of popular psychoanalysis, particularly in the form of self-help books, that a major reconstruction of the American white-collar worker took place.

Currell concentrates on Columbia Professor Walter B. Pitkin's influential best-seller *Life Begins at Forty* (1932), which addresses a middle-class readership temporarily unemployed as a consequence of the Great Depression. This, Pitkin argued, was only an interlude in a general movement towards increased leisure time and self-cultivation. Through moral and intellectual training, middle-class workers would be able to take up roles within a 'planned, rationalized, social and economic order led by the "keenest" minds.' This, in turn, would reflexively reorganize the capitalist system, which would take the rational individual as its starting point. Pitkin's books combined the personal with the political, offering a vision of a New America in which 'naturally' vigorous middle-class Americans could start again and reclaim their authority 'over their mental and social inferiors'. His vision of the future is therefore one that bears a close resemblance to Fordism in its reliance on automation and self-discipline, but within which the petite bourgeoisie have a greatly enhanced role and exercise a coercive form of domination over their subordinates. She quotes his vision of the future:

Between now and 1975, superior people will grow steadily less and less dependent upon low-grade workers. Drudgery disappears from farm and field, from mill and factory, from school and home. Super-power wipes out most of it; the rest will soon be erased by scientific organizing, by teamwork, and by inventions. Already we begin to drive out the stupid, the unskilled, and the misplaced alien, not with whips and scorn but through the kindlier method of firing him for keeps.

(cited in Currell 2006: 122)

The American tradition of therapeutic self-help literature may at times be the object of satire, but it has also been a highly exportable cultural form, spreading (and transforming) Fordist philosophies on a global scale. For Americanism-Fordism was not simply an economic doctrine but also a set of values closely associated with popular culture. Indeed, since Fordist production did not become commonplace in many European countries until after the Second World War, it is conceivable that the 'psycho-physical equilibrium' required by Fordism had to be diffused before transformations in the economy could take place. It is therefore to the export of American culture that we now turn.

AMERICANIZATION AND CULTURE

The Prison Notebooks are fragmentary and contradictory in their discussion of cultural Americanization. On the one hand, Gramsci dismisses the idea that America has produced new cultural forms, arguing that it has only 'remasticated' old European styles. Instead he poses the issue in reductive terms. Since the American economy bears an 'implacable weight', it will soon transform the material basis of European civilization, thereby bringing about 'the overthrow of the existing forms of civilization, and the forced birth of a . . . "new culture" and "new way of life"' (Gramsci 1971: 317). He has nothing to say about the precise form that this culture will take. Yet at the same time, an image of American culture as different is implicit in Gramsci's argument, for he tells us that the 'passive residues' of the European intelligentsia oppose Americanism because it offends their monopoly over tastefulness and quality. Since this group is unable to rebuild a meaningful culture, it is forced into the negative role of simply condemning any manifestation of Americanism. This would imply that American cultural forms in the period occupied a position of 'lowness' or popularity, in opposition to the 'high' or legitimate culture defended by traditional intellectual gatekeepers as evidence of their superiority.

We can extend this argument by looking at Gramsci's thoughts elsewhere on the subject of popular culture. As we have seen, Gramsci argues that the Italian intelligentsia failed to produce any tradition of popular literature during the nineteenth century, since it refused to include the popular classes in its hegemony. The Italian people therefore found their literature abroad, particularly from France, whose popular fiction resonated with their experiences and aspirations. This opened the way for Italians to be influenced by alien forms of feeling. As Gramsci notes, each nation has a literature, 'but this can come to it from another people, in other words the people in question can be subordinated to the intellectual and moral hegemony of other peoples' (Gramsci 1985: 255). In the twentieth century, those 'other peoples' were overwhelmingly American, and the popular forms through which America's hegemony were articulated were dance music (see box) and more particularly cinema. These were certainly not remasticated European culture, but technologically and aesthetically original forms.

GRAMSCI ON JAZZ

Despite his repeated demands that intellectuals must 'feel' and understand the popular, Gramsci's own judgements on twentieth-century culture were typically conservative and confused. One of his prison letters analyses jazz, which he fails to recognize as an American phenomenon, seeing it instead as the unmediated expression of black Africa. Moreover, he has difficulty acknowledging it as a truly popular form, preferring to couch it in terms of a spirit of 'negritude', which appeals to, and influences, the dilettante middle class:

> If there is a danger [of idolatry], it lies in the Negro music and dancing that has been imported into Europe. This music has completely won over a whole section of the cultured population of Europe, to the point of real fanaticism. It is inconceivable that the incessant repetition of the Negroes' physical gestures as they dance around their fetishes or that the constant sound of the syncopated rhythm of jazz bands should have no ideological effects.
>
> (Gramsci 1979: 123)

Much subsequent analysis of Americanism in Europe has concentrated less on how audiences were won for American hegemony, than how Americanization was used as a motif within national struggles for hegemony. Both O'Shea (1996) and Chambers (2000) note that British working-class audiences used Hollywood cinema as a means of transcending the limitations of their place-bound identities and contesting the power of the leading social group. While British cinema expressed an 'insular universe' dependent upon British filmmakers' traditionalist assumptions about good taste and the well-made film, Hollywood offered more 'daring visions' within which the audience could come to understand the democratic potential of modern life. Citing the American-made *The Wild One* (1953) and the British-made *Saturday Night and Sunday Morning* (1961), Chambers argues that, despite the films' shared focus on youthful male rebellion, only the former film could break with the common-sense view of the world and therefore with the ruling bloc's hegemony. The meanings of a near-mythical 'America', he concludes, 'consumerism, modernism, youth, the refusal of tradition . . . represented a more significant challenge to native cultural hegemony than more local forms of opposition based on more traditional affiliations' (Chambers 2000: 273–4).

In response to these democratic pleasures, European intellectuals undoubtedly entrenched themselves 'as if in the grip of . . . dissolution and despair'. Dick Hebdige (1988) notes the emergence of a 'negative consensus' in Britain, in which intellectuals of all political persuasions, and in many different fields, reacted in horror to the assumed 'levelling-down' of moral and cultural standards provoked by the importation of Americanized cultural forms and practices. This pessimism resonates with Chambers' argument, since one of the intellectuals' most potent images was of the British youngster who had 'gone over' to the myth-world of America through the adoption of Americanized patterns of dress, speech and viewing and listening habits.

As Hebdige makes clear, people's actual adoption of American forms and values has been much more negotiated than either the cultural democratization or cultural imperialism positions outlined above, and this might move us forward in thinking about the usefulness of Gramsci's argument. For Hebdige, although Fordism had won the argument at the level of production, through its ability to reproduce commodities on a mass scale, this did not mean that it had won the struggle for values. The accessibility of American culture certainly resonated amongst many Europeans, but in wearing jeans, watching a Hollywood movie, listening to soul music or eating a hamburger, the meanings of these things became transformed and appropriated. He therefore points out that popular taste in 1960s Britain was constructed out of a mixture of American, European and native cultural forms, which would suggest some caution is needed when thinking about the power of Americanism and the weakness of the old order. Similarly, the appearance in 1960s Italy of 'spaghetti westerns' which flouted the conventions of Hollywood film and briefly sustained the Italian film industry in the face of Hollywood domination, suggested both the penetration of American culture and the dialogue in which it found itself.

A further reason for re-evaluating, but certainly not dispensing with Gramsci's analysis is that the world economy has changed. It is frequently argued that Americanism and Fordism have been superseded by a period of globalization and post-Fordism. Yet whether we accept this as a break with the past or not, and whether or not we accept the economy to be determinant, many of the issues identified by Gramsci continue to be significant. Planned economies may have fallen out of favour, but the rationalization and massification of production has not. Ritzer's study of 'McDonaldization', for example, argues that the rationalized (and deeply Fordist) principles of fast food production have 'not only revolutionized the restaurant business, but also American society, and ultimately, the world' (Ritzer 1993: xi). Similarly, Americanized production and material culture in the form of such commodities as Coca-Cola, Levi's and Nike are widespread even in countries that manifest political and religious hostility towards the United States.

Furthermore, multinational capitalism continues to attempt a 'psycho-physical' reconstruction of the worker, whether through extending production line labour into the developing world or through new strategies of binding workers to their workplaces. Steven Logan (2002) offers a useful study of how the staff discounts given to clothing retail workers make the worker both a consumer and a brand. As one employee comments, 'I have to wear these clothes everyday to school and even if I don't say I'm working at the Gap, I still have this like, *I am a Gap girl*' (Logan 2002: 126).

Finally, rationalizing and homogenizing capitalism continues to meet resistance. In part this comes from 'passive residues' that have not withered in the manner that Gramsci predicted. But equally, we should remember the Gramsci of 'Some Notes on the Southern Question', and his injunction to subordinate classes to 'find for themselves an "original", and not "Americanised" way of living' (Gramsci 1994: 317). So, for example, European opposition to Americanized food production and retailing practices has drawn together alliances of urban and rural, emergent and residual groups. Thus the film *Mondovino* (2004), a documentary on the international wine business, shows how American capital acts in concert with the 'passive residues' of the European aristocracy to produce homogenized wine worldwide. Yet within the popular opposition to this process, alongside Communists and anti-globalization protestors, are figures whose hostility to Americanization is couched in terms of quality, tradition and territory. As Johnson *et al*. (2004: 122) note, 'the residual is not what is old and dying; it is the way in which older elements are worked into contemporary hegemonies or into social alternatives and opposition.' The residual may thus be future-oriented as well as valuable to the present.

SUMMARY

This chapter has argued that Americanism and Fordism occupy an ambiguous position within Gramsci's theory of hegemony. Though they promise to modernize production and 'streamline' class society, the intensification of economic exploitation also threatens to strengthen the power of capitalism and to further subjugate working people. Through entering into every aspect of public and private life, through the subtle exercising of 'moral coercion' over the great mass of people, and through the production of pleasure, Americanism and Fordism provided ways of thinking about the uniqueness of the twentieth century. The chapter has argued that, in modified form, these issues continue to resonate in the twenty-first century.

AFTER GRAMSCI?

INTRODUCTION

This book has, of course, been written 'after Gramsci'. The world that Gramsci analysed has changed dramatically, causing us to reassess his work and evaluate its pertinence to our own period. At some points in the book this has meant using other thinkers to theorize issues that Gramsci could not be expected to have any knowledge of. In particular, Pierre Bourdieu's explorations of taste and of the emergence of new class groupings have been shown to be invaluable additions to Gramsci's theory of hegemony.

Furthermore, the book has been written after a host of commentaries on, responses to and critiques of Gramsci's work. This 'Gramsci industry' appeared simultaneously within an array of academic subject areas, producing various Gramscis tailored to the needs of different disciplines. Gramsci's writings have therefore made sense to the extent that they have helped to make sense of other things – history, geography, film studies and so on. In its focus on culture, this book has been no different. As a consequence, there are some aspects of Gramsci's work and its subsequent uses that have only been briefly addressed here – his reflections on philosophy, for example, or on party organization (see Sassoon 1982). Nor has it considered the productive uses to which hegemonic theory has been put within international relations (see Gill 1993) or Gramsci's role in the formation of the set of ideas known as regulation theory (see Thompson 1997).

Equally, there are applications of Gramsci's work that have been very well represented. One of these is the way that hegemony opens up the possibility of studying non-class forms of antagonism within a Marxist framework. Another is the usefulness of hegemony for the study of popular culture. As I have pointed out, Gramsci only minimally addresses these themes, and it is other writers who have teased these implications out of his work. This section therefore makes more explicit the role of the neo-Gramscian tradition in opening out his work. It looks in particular at two areas: the impact of Gramsci's work on the formation of Cultural Studies in the 1970s, and the deployment of hegemonic theory in responses to new social movements in the 1980s and 1990s. Both of these applications of Gramsci's work took it as axiomatic that his key categories could, with suitable reservations and qualifications, be used outside their historic moment. However, it would be remiss to pretend that this is some kind of orthodoxy. There are other schools of thought that argue either that Gramsci should be returned to his own time and place or – a linked argument – that Gramsci's own historicism is a problem. We look at these criticisms first.

HISTORICISM

Historicism is an intellectual movement that insists on the importance of historical context to the emergence and interpretation of ideas, artefacts, social groups and cultural practices. The principal advocate of historicizing Gramsci is Richard Bellamy, who argues that Gramsci's work has been misinterpreted as a general theory of ideological power in western democracies. For Bellamy, Gramsci was reinvented by the Eurocommunist movement of the 1970s as a Marxist democrat whose work argued that socialism could develop in the industrialized liberal democracies of the west. It therefore offered a 'third way', falling between social democracy on the one hand and totalitarian communism on the other. Clearly this is not a position that Gramsci himself could have formulated, since it refers to political alignments that only solidified after the defeat of Nazi Germany in 1945. Instead it was an interpretation of his work that aimed to transcend the failure of socialism. While the export of Marxist-Leninist theory to desperately underdeveloped countries had ended in the state terrorism of Stalin and Mao, Gramsci's work seemed to offer a way of thinking about the strategies needed for revolutionary change in the countries of advanced capitalism. This meant analysing 'events and movements which [Gramsci] neither knew nor could have anticipated' (Bellamy 1994: x).

In contrast, Bellamy argues that Italy in the 1920s was one of the *least* industrialized nations in the west, with one of its most fragile liberal democracies. For Bellamy, Gramsci's theories evolved as a way of understanding Italy's relative backwardness, and of formulating revolutionary strategies specific to the country's exceptionality. He maintains that only by returning Gramsci to post-Risorgimento Italy can we discover his true value as an analyst of peripheral capitalist states (ibid.: xxviii). Misrecognition of Gramsci as a general theorist of contemporary western democracy, he claims, paradoxically ends up 'by seeming to deprive him of any contemporary interest at all' (ibid.: ix. See also Femia 1993 for a critique of Gramsci as the prophet of revolutionary democracy).

Bellamy is right to emphasize Gramsci's Italianness, but his claim that we can only get to some 'true' meaning of his work by returning it to its time and place is more questionable. One reason for this lies in Gramsci's own view of history and historicism. Unlike what Adam Morton (1999) calls Bellamy's 'austere historicism', Gramsci developed a flexible historicism that could encompass the relationship between past, present and an uncertain future. We might recall that his description of common sense is not of some fully formed and immobile philosophy, but of a series of 'disjointed and episodic' layers containing 'prejudices from all past phases of history . . . and intuitions of a future philosophy which will be that of a human race united the world over' (Gramsci 1971: 324). It is the task of criticism to unpick these elements and to direct their positive aspects towards the future. Similarly, Marxism is not a set of unchanging precepts for Gramsci, but something that can only be realized 'through the concrete study of past history through present activity to construct new history' (ibid.: 427). Morton makes the point that we can extend this argument to subsequent uses of Gramsci. It is the needs of *our* culture and period that select the 'questions, ideas and problems' that are contained within Gramsci's work (Morton 1999: 4).

Confusing the demand to historicize Gramsci is the fact that other writers have criticized his work precisely *for* its historicism. This criticism is dependent upon the specific viewpoint on historicism taken by structuralist Marxism, and in particular by the Franco-Greek political theorist Nicos Poulantzas (1936–79). For Poulantzas, historicist Marxism commits the error of subscribing to the notion of a unified dominant ideology. This ideology both creates and expresses the 'essence' of a dominant class which 'becomes the class-subject of history which through its world-view manages to permeate a social formation with its unity' (Poulantzas 1978:199).

Poulantzas is highly suspicious of the privileged role that this argument grants to consciousness. It is not the consciousness of the hegemonic class, he argues, which secures the dominated classes' 'active consent' but the 'social formation' (the specific combination of economic forces and social 'regions' such as religion and the law) at any particular historical moment. For Poulantzas, historicist Marxism is ultimately idealist in its assumption that ideas produce social and moral unity. Instead the dominant ideology *reflects* that unity, and cannot therefore be some pure expression of the mindset of the ruling social group. Among other things, the 'dominant ideology' is the outcome of unequal relationships between the classes. Hence, he argues, we can understand not only why subaltern groups take on some of the ideas of the ruling class, 'but also why this discourse [the dominant ideology] often presents elements borrowed from ways of life other than that of the dominant class' (ibid.: 209).

Poulantzas's critique of historicist Marxism may be more pertinent to the work of Gramsci's Hungarian contemporary Georg Lukács (1885–1971), for as this book has argued, Gramsci's theory of hegemony is, precisely, a reaction against some notion of an imposed dominant ideology. Not only does Gramsci separate hegemony into various 'regions' (ideological, economic, political and juridical) but his notion of hegemony as a set of transactions or negotiations shares a number of features with Poulantzas's *relational* version of ideology. To be successful, a dominant power must reach into the culture of its subalterns, but within this contact zone its ambitions and strategies will be reflexively altered. Moreover, as we have seen in the earlier discussion of traditional intellectuals, Gramsci certainly does not claim there is some simple correspondence between a dominant class and its ideology. Nor does he claim that the state – in its normal operations – is a direct expression of class power.

Gramsci may be more vulnerable to the arguments of structuralist Marxism in his (inconsistent) combination of historicism, idealism and agency. Despite his critique of Croce's idealism, and despite the caveats about the interlocking regions of hegemony noted above, Gramsci did, in fact, give ideas and thinkers a very prominent role in his account of how popular consciousness is reproduced and changed. Within his thought, ideas and intellectuals are generally tied to the state of productive forces within a particular epoch, and are therefore 'historically necessary'. Yet his frequent references to Roman Catholicism indicate that ideas might become autonomous of capitalist social and economic relations and yet still exert moral and intellectual force (Bocock 1986: 93). Similarly, Gramsci accords a high level of priority to national and regional thought and culture, which are only partially determined by prevailing economic conditions. The question is whether this culturalism is actually a problem. Gramsci himself presents it as a predicament not of philosophy but of political activity. For the proletariat to hegemonize the peasantry, it must understand and accommodate cultural forms and values that are largely alien to it. Whatever the 'idealist' origins of these groups' thoughts, the resulting bloc is appreciably distinct from any notion of an essential class consciousness.

It is therefore certainly possible to find evidence of idealism in Gramsci's writings, but equally possible to find evidence of hegemony as a 'field' of lived social relationships. The fact that – without ever resolving these issues – Gramsci tried to work through and beyond them indicates why, at a particular moment, his work was adopted as a way of settling a local epistemological difficulty.

CULTURAL STUDIES AND THE 'TURN TO GRAMSCI'

The problem in question was the impasse that Cultural Studies had reached in the early 1970s. At that time, two major schools of thought had developed within what was then a relatively new subject area. On the one hand was a body of cultural theory that was strongly influenced by currents in European thought, encompassing the work of the literary critic Roland Barthes (1915–80), the anthropologist Claude Lévi-Strauss (1908–), the psychoanalyst Jacques Lacan (1901–81) and the political philosopher Louis Althusser (1918–90). Despite their very significant differences, these thinkers and their British protégés shared a common intellectual inheritance in the work of the structural linguist Ferdinand de Saussure (1857–1913) and were therefore grouped together as structuralists. As the name implies, structuralism is interested in the deep structures or rules of phenomena, rather than the specific local forms they take. Moreover, since structuralism argues that these structures generate consciousness rather than vice versa, it is suspicious of claims for human agency and instead treats culture as an 'ideological machine' that rigidly determines people's thoughts and actions (Bennett 1986b: xii).

The other intellectual camp took its inspiration from analyses of British culture associated with the work of the literary scholar Raymond Williams (1921–88) and the historian E. P. Thompson (1924–93) (both of whom made use of Gramsci's theories, as, in fact, did Althusser). These culturalists conformed to some of the features of historicism noted above: they accepted the importance of human agency and they privileged creative practices (narratives, images, music, objects) as the means by which people 'make themselves' as a class or group. Moreover, these documentary artefacts provided the resources by which historians could recover the 'authentic' worldview of subordinate social groups, including the working class, women, and ethnic and sexual minorities. There was, as a consequence, a suspiciously neat correspondence between the culture of the people and the people themselves.

As Tony Bennett explains , this situation was compounded by a settlement of these positions within particular disciplines and with particular objects of enquiry. Thus, structuralism preponderated within the study of texts, while culturalism was more concentrated in history and sociology, and in studies of phenomena such as sport and youth subcultures. Yet despite these major differences, Bennett notes that culturalism and structuralism were, in ideological terms, mirror images of each other. Both paradigms accepted the existence of 'a dominant ideology, essentially and monolith-ically bourgeois in its characteristics, which, with varying degrees of success, is imposed from without, as an alien force, on the subordinate classes' (Bennett 1986b: xiii).

Gramsci's development of the notion of hegemony represented a major advance on this 'zero-sum' game of domination and resistance. For Bennett and his co-authors, the 'turn to Gramsci' represented two major advances in thinking about culture and society. First it meant that, in thinking about popular culture, one had to neither celebrate it as the authentic expression of popular values, nor condemn it as the servant of dominant interests. Instead culture could be seen as an arena in which 'dominant, subordinate and oppositional cultural values meet and intermingle . . . vying with one another to secure the spaces within which they can [frame and organize] popular experience and consciousness' (Bennett 1986b: xix). As a consequence, issues that had previously been seen as irredeemably 'dominant' – national identity, for example, or listening to the radio – could potentially be reclaimed for a progressive politics.

The second shift of emphasis is a critique of class essentialism. We have seen that the consciousness of a class is a mosaic, containing not simply bourgeois and proletarian values, but also other forms of identification. While for Gramsci this is largely a matter of geographic identity and religion, these are clearly not the only forms of non-class identity. Thus for Bennett et al., Gramsci's writing opens up other regions of cultural struggle for analysis. The most significant of these have been race, gender and sexuality, though Gramscian thought, with its emphasis on the 'decisive nucleus of economic activity' never suggests that these categories can float entirely free from questions of class. Instead, the task of critical analysis is to consider 'the complex and changing ways in which these [phenomena] may be overlapped on one another in different historical circumstances' (Bennett 1986b: xvi).

So far in the book we have seen some of the consequences of this shift in orientation in the work of a number of British Cultural Studies scholars, and particularly those associated with the Birmingham Centre for Contemporary Cultural Studies (CCCS). Major CCCS projects discussed earlier in the body of this book have been Hebdige's *Subculture: the Meaning of Style* (1979), Hall and Jefferson's *Resistance through Rituals* (1976), Hall *et al.*'s *Policing the Crisis* (1978) and a less straightforwardly Gramscian analysis, Willis's *Learning to Labour* (1977). To these studies we can add two more projects, both shaped by the work of Stuart Hall, who has been the single most influential figure in adapting and disseminating Gramsci's ideas within studies of contemporary culture.

The first of these strands is Television Studies, which has attempted an ethnographic understanding of exactly how (and how far) audiences give their consent to the ideas of the governing classes. The stimulus for this was Hall's seminal article 'Encoding/Decoding' (1973), which argues that although television addresses its viewers as a (national) mass, the audience is actually heterogeneous. It is a mixture of social groups, of all of which are differently positioned in relation to 'dominant' ideological forms and meanings. The ideological 'message' as it is produced and transmitted (or 'encoded') by programme makers is therefore unlikely to be the same one received or 'decoded' by viewers, since their social situations and cultural values are likely to be at least slightly discrepant from dominant meanings. Hall suggests that we can discriminate such responses into three hypothetical positions – the 'preferred' (or dominant) reading, an entirely 'oppositional' reading and a 'negotiated' position. As John Fiske (1992: 126) notes, this last position is logically the most common one, since a medium like television can only be popular 'if it is open enough to admit a range of negotiated readings through which various social groups can find meaningful articulations of their own relationship to the dominant ideology'. Such a view coheres with Gramsci's view of hegemony as a process of negotiation.

Hall's encoding/decoding model has been most thoroughly used and evaluated in the work of David Morley, who has argued that Cultural Studies should attempt to devise the means of understanding how a person actively produces 'meanings from the restricted range of cultural resources which his or her structural position has allowed them access to' (1986: 43). Morley's own television ethnographies (1980, 1986, 1992) have forcefully argued against the notion that we can 'read off' people's responses to television through close analysis of the programmes themselves. Increasingly drawn to the domestic contexts within which people watch (or don't watch) television, Morley adds the crucial observation that television research needs to consider negotiations and struggles over television use (for example, over control of the handset) as much as the acceptance or rejection of screened values.

A second major strand within Hall's work has built on the analysis of political culture introduced in *Policing the Crisis*. We saw in Key Idea 7 how the 'crisis' of the 1960s resulted in an increasing adoption of coercive measures by the state during the following decade. This authoritarian drift reached its zenith with Margaret Thatcher's period as Conservative Party leader between 1975 and 1990. Hall cautiously acknowledges that 'Thatcherism' (a project by no means reducible to Mrs Thatcher herself) was successful in its ability to construct a new national-popular discourse with a wide range of points of popular contact. Thatcherism was thus a passive revolution with a difference. Although it involved almost no redistribution of power or wealth (indeed, quite the opposite), it made unprecedented efforts to speak in a populist language that invoked and engaged 'the people'. In place of the idea of the people as clients of the welfare state, Thatcherism addressed them as (potential) property owners, shareholders, entrepreneurs and consumers. This populist appeal was stitched together with old and new Conservative themes. Traditional entreaties to nation, duty and authority were joined with the 'aggressive themes of a revived neo-liberalism – self-interest, competitive individualism' (Hall 1988: 157) in a formation to which Hall gives the name *authoritarian populism*. It is, he argues, a form of 'regressive modernization', regressive because its points of reference were often backwards – to the British Empire, to the Victorians, to the Second World War – but modernizing in its role of facilitating the reconstruction and intensification of national, and particularly global, capitalism.

Substantiating Hall's contention that Thatcherism represented a fundamental (though uneven, contradictory and partial) transformation in British political and cultural life, the issues first identified in the late 1970s mutated rather than disappeared beneath the Labour landslide of 1997. As subsequent neo-Gramscian analyses of 'Blairism', particularly in the journal *Soundings*, have shown, the common sense of welfarist social democracy has continued to be 'dis-organized' by political 'modernizers'. At the same time, authoritarian ideological motifs concerning, for example, immigration and terrorism persist within our period. While this analysis is pessimistic in its acknowledgement of the mutable-while-durable nature of the hegemonic bloc, it also contains a degree of optimism in its advocacy of the shifting nature of counter-hegemony. We examine this, and its philosophical under-pinnings, in the following section.

NEW TIMES, NEW SOCIAL MOVEMENTS

The journal *Marxism Today* made one of the first uses of 'Thatcherism' in 1978. In 1988 the same journal attempted to define the cultural and political shifts that had taken place in the intervening decade under the heading 'New Times'. The phrase attempted to capture the diversity of the period, encom-passing the success of Thatcherism, the gradual dissolution of the Soviet bloc, the mutation of work and the working class, and the emergence of identity politics and consumerism as key cultural themes and developments within IT, leisure and the media (McRobbie 1991: 2). While these issues were of intrinsic interest, the New Times discourse largely couched them in terms of their significance for the Left: the success of neo-conservatism in Britain and America, it claimed, exploited failures of imagination and organization on the part of the Left.

As John Clarke (1991) explains it, two elements of New Right ideology stand out as markers of the Left's failure: its anti-statism (more accurately its anti-welfare statism) and its occupancy of a language of 'choice'. Together these genuinely popular strands captured and reinflected traditional left opposition to the bureaucratism, centralism and vested professional interest of the social democratic state. New Times, for Clarke, was an attempt to reclaim these motifs as 'good sense' by showing how choice, difference and anti-statism could be central to progressive politics. At the heart of this shift was a fundamental break with the past: the working class and its political representatives in the trade unions and in social democratic and socialist parties could no longer be depicted as the sole engine of progress. 'The changing composition of class', he writes, 'together with the emergence of new social subjects with diverse political agendas means rethinking the basis of counter-hegemonic politics, in which class is, at best, one of many identities' (Clarke 1991: 159).

The major 'rethinking' of Gramsci's work in the light of these devel-opments is Ernesto Laclau and Chantal Mouffe's *Hegemony and Socialist*

Strategy (1985). Declaring themselves 'post-Marxists', Laclau and Mouffe argue that the Left is in crisis as a consequence of its outdated faith in the working class as a 'universal' class that can liberate everyone. For them, Gramsci's theory of hegemony is an essential move forward since it establishes the principle that politics involves articulation, or, in their term, a 'logic of the social', within which discrete subject positions and social groups in a particular historical conjuncture will be bound together into a historical bloc. In modern societies, there has been a proliferation of such groups and identities, including feminism, ethnic and sexual minority rights, and the anti-war and green movements. No Left politics could ignore these struggles, but nor could they exist independently of a Left. Thus, they argue that 'the political meaning of a local community movement, of an ecological struggle, of a sexual minority movement' cannot be contained within these issues alone. Instead, 'it crucially depends upon its hegemonic articulation with other struggles and demands' (Laclau and Mouffe 1985: 87).

Laclau and Mouffe's original use of Gramscian theory represents an important contribution to an understanding of how hegemony might operate in modern democracies. As we have seen, an expansive hegemony must reach out to an array of social groups, and Laclau and Mouffe are rightly critical of separatist and millenarian projects that can only conceive of politics in terms of binary antagonisms. Nor are they convinced that new social movements are inherently progressive. Developing Gramsci's notion of the opposition between common sense and good sense, they argue that 'new social movements exist in multiple forms which may be shaped through hegemonic struggle to progressive or reactionary ends'. No emergent movement can be 'absolutely radical and irrecuperable for the dominant order, [none] constitutes an absolutely guaranteed point of departure for a total transformation' (ibid.: 169). Moreover they observe that Marxism has drastically limited its imagination of politics through granting political parties and the state a vital role. Many manifestations of feminism, for example, 'transform the relationship between masculinity and femininity without passing through parties or the State' (ibid.: 153).

Although these observations are indebted to hegemonic theory, Laclau and Mouffe break decisively with Gramsci in making two linked claims: first, that there cannot be one hegemonic pole within a political formation, and second that an individual or group's political interests are entirely constructed through the process of articulation. While we can see some licence for this latter conclusion in Gramsci's work, Laclau and Mouffe radically inflate his sense of constructing a new common sense, until it breaks free of any mooring in an individual or group's social position. In a scathing review of their work, Terry Eagleton (1991) has pointed out that this suggests no logical impediment to men leading a feminist struggle or capitalists a socialist one. Yet it is unquestionably women who have most to gain from feminism, and the working class from socialism. It is, writes Eagleton, 'in this sense that the relation between certain social locations and certain political forms is a "necessary" one – which is not to assert that it is inevitable, guaranteed or God-given' (Eagleton 1991: 218). By contrast, Laclau and Mouffe's position on political engagement sounds very much like the 'voluntarist' tendency that Gramsci warns against, in which politics becomes simply a matter of choice.

Laclau and Mouffe's rejection of the idea of a leading group *within* a bloc also raises some questions. We should bear in mind that they are overwhelmingly concerned with *counter*-hegemonic politics, and therefore make only a perfunctory gesture towards the hegemonic strategies of 'dominant' groups. But it seems curious to treat hegemony in this way, not least because, at the very time they were writing, radical Right projects such as Thatcherism aimed to demobilize and dis-organize the Left, articulating some 'subaltern' groups to it in the process. It is as if dominant groups play one game of hegemony, and subordinate groups another! Indeed, Laclau and Mouffe's definition of hegemony seems oddly un-Gramscian, since they treat it as a synonym for 'federation' rather than as a way of conceiving how one group exerts moral and intellectual leadership over another. Hegemony comes to be a statement of an ideal, rather than a tool of analysis, or indeed of strategy, since it is difficult to see who would provide the leadership of a struggle, or what issues would form a 'decisive nucleus'.

As John Clarke (1991) has noted, dealing with post-Marxism more generally, this utopianism leads to some notable evasions. In particular, hegemony is reduced to a matter of ideological (or, for Laclau and Mouffe, 'symbolic') conflict, rather than a process simultaneously carried out in the material realm, in civil society and in the state. The idealist notion of a free association of progressive forces has, for Clarke, been somewhat undermined by the ruling bloc's ability to reshape the conditions under which opposition can take place by such strategies as, for example, controlling social benefits, limiting educational opportunities or restricting trade union membership. Similarly, as Robert Bocock (1986) argues, Laclau and Mouffe are simply too dismissive of economic issues as one issue amongst many. One of the reasons the capitalist system of production has been so successful is that it provides an expansive organizing principle that reaches into all areas of social life across the globe. Laclau and Mouffe's claim that 'socialism is one of the components of a project for radical democracy, not vice versa' (1985: 16) is therefore not quite as obvious as they assume.

Alongside their post-Marxism, it is fair to characterize Laclau and Mouffe, together with their real mentor Michel Foucault (1926–84), as post-structuralists. By this, I mean a group of thinkers who share a scepticism towards 'universal' truths, towards the idea that power is uniformly inflicted *upon* people, and towards a faith in 'totalizing' positivist projects. It should be immediately obvious from the tenor of this book that these are per-spectives that may also be encountered in *The Prison Notebooks*. The question, therefore, is the extent to which Gramsci's work may be reconciled with post-Marxism, post-structuralism and their intellectual acquaintances post-modernism and post-Fordism.

Some thinkers have tried to reconcile Gramsci with these intellectual movements. Marcia Landy (1994), for example, has attempted to show the high level of correlation between Gramsci's work and that of Antonio Negri (1933–) who, with his co-author Michael Hardt, has been one of the key theorists of post-Fordism. Renata Holub (1992), going somewhat further, has argued that Gramsci's work gestures to a point of reconciliation 'beyond Marxism and postmodernism'. It is perfectly understandable to see Gramscian Marxism (if not Gramsci himself) as sharing conceptual ground with these 'Posts', where, 'though classes still exist there is no guaranteed dynamic to class struggle and no 'class belonging' and where 'no one "owns" an ideology because ideologies are themselves in process: in a state of constant formation and reformation' (Hebdige 1988: 206). Yet, as Dick Hebdige acknowledges, Marxism has not been dissolved into the 'Posts'. Gramsci's idiosyncratic form of socialism is not, finally, a form of relativism in which all struggles are equal. Nor can it depart from the idea of an ongoing struggle for change, by working men and women acting in concert against the organized, durable and global system of exploitation and oppression that is capitalism.

To make this point is not to argue for an unchanging Marxism. Gramsci's contribution to Marxist theory lies precisely in its argument that socialists must pay attention to the contingent and conjunctural features of an epoch, to be 'scholars of vulgar wisdom' who are attentive to the currents of their age. Playing with Gramsci's opposition between intellectual pessimism and the need for optimism, Hebdige argues that, despite all predictions of its demise, democratic Marxism has survived. It is a fittingly Gramscian conclusion to this book:

Marxism has 'gone under' in a succession of tempests . . . and yet it is a marxism that has survived, returning perhaps a little lighter on its feet (staggering at first), a marxism more prone perhaps to listen, learn, adapt and to appreciate, for instance, that words like 'emergency' and 'struggle' don't just mean fight, conflict, war and death but birthing, the prospect of new life emerging, a struggling to the light.

(Hebdige 1988: 207)

FURTHER READING

WORKS BY ANTONIO GRAMSCI IN ENGLISH

The first text that a reader should engage with is undoubtedly *The Prison Notebooks*. However, some scholars feel that the very editing and translation of the *Notebooks* constitute a question for analysis. Perry Anderson, for example, describes it as 'a work censored twice over: its spaces, ellipses, contradictions, disorders, allusions, repetitions, are the result of its uniquely adverse process of composition' and warns against 'facile and complacent readings' based on partial editions of his work (Anderson 1976: 6). Without doubt, the publication of a complete critical edition of the *Notebooks* has been a slow process. The first Italian edition, brought out in six volumes between 1948 and 1951 by the Turin publisher Einaudi, abridged Gramsci's copious prison writings and organized them into a series of themes chosen by the editor, Felice Platone.

Einaudi's format, supplemented by some original reference to Gramsci's manuscripts, was followed by the main English translation, *Selections from the Prison Notebooks*, edited and translated by Quintin Hoare and Geoffrey Nowell-Smith (1971). I have largely followed Hoare and Nowell-Smith's translation during the writing of this book, using the edition published by Lawrence & Wishart, which contains a number of useful introductory essays. The *Selections* is also available as a CD-ROM published by Electronic Book Classics (ElecBook). *Further Selections from the Prison Notebooks*, edited and translated by Derek Boothman, was published by both the University of Minnesota Press and Lawrence & Wishart in 1995 and may be found on the same CD as the *Selections*.

For the serious scholar, a critical edition of the entire *Prison Notebooks*, translated by Antonio Callari and edited by Joseph A. Buttigieg, is currently in production. It is based on the first complete Italian edition of the *Notebooks*, edited by Valentino Gerratana in 1975 and again published by Einaudi. Volume 1 of Buttigieg's edition appeared in 1992, containing Notebooks 1 and 2 (of the 29 original notebooks), and Volume 2, which contains Notebooks 3, 4, and 5, was published in 1996. Volume 3 is scheduled for publication in 2006. All volumes are published by Columbia University Press.

Gramsci's writings, however, were not limited to the *Notebooks*. He was a prolific political journalist, arts critic and letter writer, and various volumes gather these different Gramscis together. His *Pre-Prison Writings* have been translated by Virginia Cox and edited by Richard Bellamy, who also contributes a challenging and stimulating essay, arguing that too much concentration on the *Notebooks* deflects attention away from Gramsci as a political activist and theorist of uneven development. It was published by Cambridge University Press in 1994.

A selection of Gramsci's *Letters from Prison*, revealing not only the conditions of his imprisonment but also his thoughts on topics including psychoanalysis and jazz, was edited by Lynne Lawner, who also contributed a useful essay on the main currents of Gramsci's life and thought. It was first published by Harper & Row in 1973. A more complete, two-volume edition of the *Letters* was published by Columbia University Press in 1994, translated by Raymond Rosenthal and edited by Frank Rosengarten, who provides an introduction.

Lawrence & Wishart published a selection of Gramsci's *Cultural Writings*, edited and introduced by David Forgacs and Geoffrey Nowell-Smith, in 1985. It contains theatrical and literary criticism (including sustained analyses of Pirandello's plays and Dante's *Divine Comedy*), essays on journalism and critical analysis of Catholic and Fascist cultural production (grouped together as 'Father Bresciani's Progeny'). It also contains sections on such key concepts as popular literature, folklore, 'national-popular' and cultural Americanization. Forgacs also edited *The Antonio Gramsci Reader*, covering the whole period from 1916 to 1935, which might be an alternative first port of call. It was first published by Schocken Books, NY, in 1988, with a later UK edition by Lawrence & Wishart appearing in 1999.

BIOGRAPHIES

This book has used Giuseppe Fiori's accessible and anecdotal *Antonio Gramsci: Life of a Revolutionary*, first published in Italian in 1965 and translated by Tom Nairn for New Left Books in 1970. You may also wish to read Alastair Davidson's *Antonio Gramsci: Towards an Intellectual Biography*, first published by the Merlin Press in 1977.

INTRODUCTORY STUDIES OF GRAMSCI

There are a number of introductory texts available on Gramsci's work. Good first stops, though both now quite old, and both more concerned with politics than culture, are *Gramsci* by James Joll (Fontana, 1977) and *Gramsci's Political Thought: An Introduction* by Roger Simon (Lawrence & Wishart, 1982). Later editions of this latter book contain a superb short essay by Stuart Hall, and the whole volume is included on the ElecBook CD-ROM mentioned earlier.

A more challenging and rewarding introduction is Paul Ransome's *Antonio Gramsci: A New Introduction* (Harvester Wheatsheaf, 1992). Although again primarily concerned with politics, this is an admirably clear piece of writing whose structure is very student-friendly. An introductory essay charts the various seasons of Gramsci studies and makes the case for Gramsci's continuing centrality to social and political thinking.

MORE ADVANCED AND SPECIALIST STUDIES

For general studies of Gramsci, Robert Bocock's short book *Hegemony* (Tavistock Press, 1986) is a clear and concise introduction to the subject, rooting it clearly in the Marxist tradition and also providing a useful synopsis of Laclau and Mouffe (1985). Chantal Mouffe's edited collection of essays, *Gramsci and Marxist Theory* (1979) contains not only a useful introduction by Mouffe herself, but also the essays by Norberto Bobbio ('Gramsci and the Conception of Civil Society') and Jacques Texier ('Gramsci, Theoretician of the Superstructures') referred to in Key Idea 2. For the serious scholar, around 80 essays, many of which are classics of Gramsci studies, can be found in the four volumes of *Antonio Gramsci: Critical Assessments of Leading Political Philosophers* edited by James Martin and published by Routledge in 2002.

For the application of Gramsci to textual studies, the collection *Popular Fictions* edited by Peter Humm, Paul Stigant and Peter Widdowson (Methuen, 1986) contains some Gramscian approaches, while Christine Gledhill's essay 'Pleasurable Negotiations' in *Female Spectators* (ed. E. Deirdre Pribram, Verso, 1988) is useful for both television drama and feminist uses of Gramsci. The most sustained textual approach is Marcia Landy's *Film, Politics and Gramsci* (University of Minnesota Press, 1994). Although this can be slow-going, there are some fruitful attempts to apply Gramsci to various national film cycles, and a useful essay mapping the correspondences between Gramsci and Antonio Negri's work.

In terms of the relationship between Gramsci and post-modernism, the case for and against is set out in Renata Holub's *Antonio Gramsci: Beyond Marxism and Postmodernism* (Routledge, 1992). However, a better starting point may be Ernesto Laclau and Chantal Mouffe's *Hegemony and Socialist Strategy* (Verso, 1985), discussed in the previous chapter. This has been the single most significant revision of hegemonic theory in recent times.

For Gramsci's use in Cultural Studies, see Tony Bennett, Colin Mercer and Janet Woollacott's *Popular Culture and Social Relations* (Open University Press, 1986), which charts the moment of the 'Turn to Gramsci', together with some useful interpretations of popular culture. Some of Stuart Hall's uses of Gramsci, including the important essay 'Gramsci's Relevance for the Study of Race and Ethnicity' and articles on New Times are collected in *Stuart Hall: Critical Dialogues in Cultural Studies*, edited by David Morley and Kuan-Hsing Chen (Routledge, 1996). Finally, the case against can be found in David Harris's self-explanatory *From Class Struggle to the Politics of Pleasure: the Effects of Gramscianism on Cultural Studies* (Routledge, 1992).

INTERNET RESOURCES

There are many internet sites on the works of Antonio Gramsci and these can be accessed by typing 'Gramsci' into a search engine. Some of the more curious uses and abuses of his writings can be found by this scatter-gun approach. As Marcus Green (2000) notes, a number of articles by right-wing web authors present Gramsci as a Machiavellian figure, plotting from beyond the grave to provoke a 'culture war' in the United States! More sober assessments of his work, bibliographies and Gramsci resources may be found on the following sites:

http://www.italnet.nd.edu/gramsci/

The website of the International Gramsci Society, this houses a mass of material, including biographical and chronological information about Gramsci, photographs relating to him, a documentary film, back copies of the excellent *International Gramsci Society Newsletter*, essays and web links. It is the most comprehensive website devoted to Gramsci.

http://www.victoryiscertain.com/gramsci/

An eclectic and informal set of links to all sorts of material: Gramsci's writings on-line, the aforementioned right-wing and religious appropriations of Gramsci and essays on his work.

http://www.gramsci.it/

The website of the Fondazione Istituto Gramsci. It includes the most comprehensive bibliography of work on Gramsci, the *Bibliografia Gramsciana*, which covers writings in over 30 languages. The main bibliography goes up to 1988, with supplements covering subsequent publications. It can also be accessed, via an English-language site at: http://www.soc.qc.edu/gramsci/index.html

WORKS CITED

Anderson, P. (1976) 'The Antinomies of Antonio Gramsci', *New Left Review*, 100.

Barker, M. (1992) *'Policing the Crisis'* in M. Barker and A. Beezer (eds) *Reading into Cultural Studies*, London: Routledge.

BBC (2004a) http://www.bbc.co.uk/northamptonshire/features/2004/st_georges_day. Accessed 24 April 2004.

—— (2004b) http://www.bbc.co.uk/london/yourlondon/stgeorges/ Accessed 24 April 2004.

Bellamy, R. (1987) *Modern Italian Social Theory: Ideology and Politics from Pareto to the Present*, Cambridge: Polity.

—— (1994) 'Introduction' in A. Gramsci, *Antonio Gramsci: Pre-Prison Writings*, Cambridge: Cambridge University Press.

Bennett, T. (1986a) 'Hegemony, Ideology, Pleasure: Blackpool', in T. Bennett, C. Mercer and J. Woollacott (eds) *Popular Culture and Social Relations*, Buckingham: Open University Press.

—— (1986b) 'Popular Culture and the Turn to Gramsci' in T. Bennett, C. Mercer and J. Woollacott (eds) *Popular Culture and Social Relations*, Buckingham: Open University Press.

Bennett, T. and Woollacott, J. (1987) *Bond and Beyond: The Political Career of a Popular Hero*, Basingstoke: Macmillan.

Bobbio, N. (1979) 'Gramsci and the Conception of Civil Society' in C. Mouffe (ed.) *Gramsci and Marxist Theory*, London: Routledge.

Bocock, R. (1986) *Hegemony*, London: Tavistock.

Bourdieu, P. (1984) *Distinction: A Social Critique of the Judgement of Taste*, London: Routledge.

—— (1997) 'The Economy of Practices' in K. Woodward (ed.) *Identity and Difference*, London: SAGE.

Buchanan, P. (2000) 'Note Sulla "Escuola Italiana": Using Gramsci in the Current International Moment', *Contemporary Politics*, 6, 2.

Buci-Glucksmann, C. (1982) 'Hegemony and Consent' in A. Showstack Sassoon (ed.) *Approaches to Gramsci*, London: Writers and Readers.

Chambers, I. (2000) 'Gramsci Goes to Hollywood' in J. Hollows, P. Hutchings and M. Jancovich (eds) *The Film Studies Reader*, London: Arnold.

Chaney, D. (2002) *Cultural Change and Everyday Life*, Basingstoke: Palgrave.

Clarke, J. (1991) *New Times and Old Enemies: Essays on Cultural Studies and America*, London: HarperCollins.

Cohen, P. (1980) 'Subcultural Conflict and Working-Class Community', in S. Hall, D. Hobson, A. Lowe and P. Willis (eds) *Culture, Media, Language: Working Papers in Cultural Studies, 1972–79*, London: Hutchinson.

Currell, S. (2006) 'Depression and Recovery: Self-help and America in the Great Depression', in D. Bell and J. Hollows (eds) *Historicizing Lifestyles*, Aldershot: Ashgate.

Davidson, A. (1977) *Antonio Gramsci: Towards an Intellectual Biography*, London: Merlin Press.

Deal, T. and Kennedy, A. (1982) *Corporate Cultures*, Harmondsworth: Penguin.

Douglas, M. (1966) *Purity and Danger: an Analysis of Concepts of Pollution and Taboo*, London: Routledge.

Downey, J. and Fenton, N. (2003) 'New Media, Counter Publicity and the Public Sphere', *New Media and Society*, 5, 2.

du Gay, P. (1991) 'Enterprise Culture and the Ideology of Excellence', *New Formations*, 13.

—— (1997) 'Organizing Identity: Making up People at Work' in P. du Gay (ed.) *Production of Culture / Cultures of Production*, London: SAGE.

du Gay, P., Hall, S., Janes, L., Mackay, H. and Negus, K. (1997) *Doing Cultural Studies: the Story of the Sony Walkman*, London: SAGE.

Eagleton, T. (1991) *Ideology: An Introduction*, London: Verso.

Femia, J. (1993) *Marxism and Democracy*, Oxford: Clarendon Press.

Fiori, G. (1970) *Antonio Gramsci, Life of a Revolutionary*, tr. T. Nairn, London: New Left Books.

Fiske, J. (1992) 'British Cultural Studies and Television' in R. Allen (ed.) *Channels of Discourse*, London: Routledge.

Forgacs, D. (1993) 'National-Popular: Genealogy of a Concept' in S. During (ed.) *The Cultural Studies Reader*, London: Routledge.

Germino, D. (1990) *Antonio Gramsci: Architect of a New Politics*, Baton Rouge: Louisiana State University Press.

Gill, S. (ed.) (1993) *Gramsci, Historical Materialism and International Relations*, Cambridge: Cambridge University Press.

Gilroy, P. (1987) *There Ain't No Black in the Union Jack*, London: Unwin Hyman.

Gledhill, C. (1988) 'Pleasurable Negotiations' in E. Pribram (ed.) *Female Spectators*, London: Verso.

Gramsci, A. (1971) *Selections from the Prison Notebooks*, London: Lawrence & Wishart.

—— (1979) *Letters from Prison by Antonio Gramsci*, London: Quartet.

—— (1985) *Selections from the Cultural Writings*, London: Lawrence & Wishart.

—— (1994) *Antonio Gramsci: Pre-Prison Writings*, Cambridge: Cambridge University Press.

—— (1995) *Further Selections from the Prison Notebooks*, Minneapolis: University of Minnesota Press.

Gray, A. (2003) 'Enterprising Femininity: New Modes of Work and Subjectivity', *European Journal of Cultural Studies*, 6, 4.

Green, M. (2000) 'Gramsci on the World Wide Web: Intellectuals and Bizarre Interpretations of Gramsci', *International Gramsci Society Newsletter*, 10.

Hall, S. (1973/1980) 'Encoding/Decoding' in Centre for Contemporary Cultural Studies (ed.) *Culture, Media, Language: Working Papers in Cultural Studies, 1929–79*, London: Hutchinson.

Hall, S. (1988) *The Hard Road to Renewal: Thatcherism and the Crisis of the Left*, London: Verso.

—— (1990) 'Cultural Identity and Diaspora' in J. Rutherford (ed.) *Identity: Community, Culture, Difference*, London: Lawrence & Wishart.

—— (1996) 'Gramsci's Relevance for the Study of Race and Ethnicity' in D. Morley and K.-H. Chen (eds) *Stuart Hall: Critical Dialogues in Cultural Studies*, London: Routledge.

Hall, S. and Jefferson, T. (1976) *Resistance through Rituals: Youth Subcultures in Post-War Britain*, London: Hutchinson.

Hall, S., Critcher, C., Jefferson, T., Clarke, J. and Roberts, B. (1978) *Policing the Crisis: Mugging, the State, and Law and Order*, London: Macmillan.

Hebdige, D. (1979) *Subculture: The Meaning of Style*, London: Methuen.

—— (1988) *Hiding in the Light: on Images and Things*, London: Comedia.

Higson, A. (1995) *Waving the Flag: Constructing a National Cinema in Britain*, Oxford: Oxford University Press.

Hill, C. (1947) *Lenin and the Russian Revolution*, London: English Universities Press.

Hollows, J. (2002) *Feminism, Femininity and Popular Culture*, Manchester: Manchester University Press.

—— (2003) 'Oliver's Twist: Leisure, Labour and Domestic Masculinity in The Naked Chef", *International Journal of Cultural Studies*, 6, 2.

Holst, J. (1999) 'The Affinities of Lenin and Gramsci: Implications for Radical Adult Education Theory and Practice', *International Journal of Lifelong Education*, 18, 5.

Holub, R. (1992) *Antonio Gramsci: Beyond Marxism and Postmodernism*, London: Routledge.

Howell, J. and Ingham, A. (2001) 'From Social Problem to Personal Issue: the Language of Lifestyle', *Cultural Studies*, 15, 2.

Hunt, L. (1997) *British Low Culture: From Safari Suits to Sexploitation*, London: Routledge.

—— (1999) 'Dog Eat Dog' in S. Chibnall and R. Murphy (eds) *British Crime Cinema*, London: Routledge.

Hurd, G. (ed.) (1984) *National Fictions: World War Two in British Films and Television*, London: British Film Institute.

Hutton, W. (2004) 'Can We Trust our Officer Class?' *Observer*, 30 May.

Johnson, R., Chambers, D., Raghuram, P. and Tincknell, E. (2004) *The Practice of Cultural Studies*, London: SAGE.

Laclau, E. and Mouffe, C. (1985) *Hegemony and Socialist Strategy: Towards a Radical Democratic Politics*, London: Verso.

Landy, M. (1994) *Film, Politics and Gramsci*, Minneapolis: University of Minnesota Press.

Lawner, L. (1979) 'Introduction' in A. Gramsci (1979) *Letters from Prison by Antonio Gramsci*, London: Quartet.

Lee, M. (1993) *Consumer Culture Reborn: The Cultural Politics of Consumption*, London: Routledge.

Livingstone, S. and Lunt, P. (1994) *Talk on Television*, London: Routledge.

Lo Piparo, F. (1979) *Lingua, Intellettuali, Egemonia in Gramsci*, Bari: Laterza.

Logan, S. (2002) 'Everyone in Leather: Work and Play in the Corporate Culture of The Gap', *Critical Sense*, X, 1. Available at http://criticalsense.berkeley.edu/. Accessed 25 August 2005.

Machiavelli, N. (1988) *The Prince*, Cambridge: Cambridge University Press.

McRobbie, A. (1991) 'New Times in Cultural Studies', *New Formations*, 13.

Marx, K. (1977) *Karl Marx: Selected Writings*, ed. D. McLellan, Oxford: Oxford University Press.

Mercer, C. (1984) 'Generating Consent', *Ten.8*, 18.

Moores, S. (2000) *Media and Everyday Life in Modern Society*, Edinburgh: Edinburgh University Press.

Morley, D. (1980) *'The "Nationwide" Audience: Structure and Decoding*, London: British Film Institute.

—— (1986) *Family Television: Cultural Power and Domestic Leisure*, London: Comedia.

—— (1992) *Television, Audiences and Cultural Studies*, London: Routledge.

Morton, A. (1999) 'On Gramsci', *Politics*, 19, 1.

Moss, S. (2004) 'Labour MP Gets Set to Fight St. George's Corner', *Guardian*, 23 April.

Nixon, S. (1997) 'Circulating Culture' in P. du Gay (ed.) *Production of Culture/Cultures of Production*, London: SAGE.

O'Shea, Alan (1996) 'English Subjects of Modernity' in M. Nava and A. O'Shea (eds) *Modern Times: Reflections on a Century of English Modernity*, London: Routledge.

Poulantzas, N. (1978) *Political Power and Social Classes*, London: Verso.

Probyn, E. (2000) *Carnal Appetites: Foodsexidentities*, London: Routledge.

Ransome, P. (1992) *Antonio Gramsci: A New Introduction*, Hemel Hempstead: Harvester Wheatsheaf.

Ritzer, G. (1993) *The McDonaldization of Society*, London: SAGE.

Robinson, J. (2005) 'Reality Bites for the BBC', *Observer*, 6 March.

Rose, T. (1994) *Black Noise: Rap Music and Black Culture in Contemporary America*, Hanover: Wesleyan University Press.

Ross, A. (1989) *No Respect: Intellectuals and Popular Culture*, London: Routledge.

—— (1995) 'The Great White Dude' in M. Berger, B. Wallis and S. Watson (eds) *Constructing Masculinity*, London: Routledge.

Salaman, G. (1997) 'Culturing Production', in P. du Gay (ed.) *Production of Culture/Cultures of Production*, London: SAGE.

Sassoon, A. Showstack (ed. 1982) *Approaches to Gramsci*, London: Writers and Readers.

—— (1999) *Gramsci and Contemporary Politics*, London: Routledge.

Simon, R. (1982) *Gramsci's Political Thought: An Introduction*, London: Lawrence & Wishart.

Skeggs, B. (1992) 'Paul Willis, *Learning to Labour*' in M. Barker and A. Beezer (eds) *Reading Into Cultural Studies*, London: Routledge.

Stabile, C. (2001) Conspiracy or Consensus? Reconsidering the Moral Panic', *Journal of Communication Inquiry*, 25, 3.

Strinati, D. (1995) *An Introduction to Theories of Popular Culture*, London: Routledge.

Texier, J. (1979) 'Gramsci, Theoretician of the Superstructures' in C. Mouffe (ed.) *Gramsci and Marxist Theory*, London: Routledge.

Thompson, K. (ed.) (1997) *Media and Cultural Regulation*, London: SAGE.

Urbinati, N. (1998) 'The Souths of Antonio Gramsci and the Concept of Hegemony' in J. Schneider (ed.) *Italy's 'Southern Question': Orientalism in One Country*, Oxford: Berg.

Wiener, M. (1981) *English Culture and the Decline of the Industrial Spirit, 1850–1980*, Cambridge: Cambridge University Press.

Williams, R. (1980) *Problems in Materialism and Culture*, London: Verso.

Williamson, J. (1991) '"Up Where You Belong": Hollywood images of big business in the 1980s', in J. Corner and S. Harvey (eds) *Enterprise and Heritage: Crosscurrents of National Culture*, London: Routledge.

Willis, A. (1995) 'Cultural Studies and Popular Film' in J. Hollows and M. Jancovich (eds) *Approaches to Popular Film*, Manchester: Manchester University Press.

Willis, P. (1977) *Learning to Labour: How Working Class Kids Get Working Class Jobs*, Farnborough: Saxon House.

Wilmott, H. (1997) 'Symptoms of Resistance' in P. du Gay (ed.) *Production of Culture/Cultures of Production*, London: SAGE.

INDEX

Action Party 14, 15, 52, 98
Adorno, Theodor 48
agency 46, 81; privileging of over
   structure 81
Althusser, Louis 34, 125
Americanism–Fordism 109–20; and
   culture 116–19; and 'parasitic'
   class 110–11; workers' morality
   and pleasure 112–16, 120
anti-positivism 18
aristocracy, English 88–9
army, British 51
authoritarian populism 128
authoritarianism 101
avant-gardism 67, 70
Avanti! 20, 21

'backlash' movies 98
Barthes, Roland 125
Bartoli, Matteo 18, 35
base–superstructure relationship
   27–30, 33–4, 39
BBC (British Broadcasting
   Corporation) 5–6, 7, 9, 77–9
Bellamy, Richard 22, 44, 122, 123
Bennett, Tony 53, 71, 82, 126

big business 72–3
black intellectuals 84
Blackpool 53
Blairism 128–9
Bobbio, Norberto 34
Bocock, Robert 131
Bohemianism 114
Bolsheviks 21, 31
Bonapartism 99, 100
Bond, James 71–2
Bordiga, Amadeo 23, 30
Bourdieu, Pierre 52, 121; *Distinction*
   86
bourgeoisie 43, 44, 100; petite 86–7,
   114, 115
Britain 38–9; and Americanization of
   culture 117–18; 'mugging panic'
   (1970s)
102, 104; and *Policing the Crisis* 102–5;
   working-class movement 52–3
British Board of Film Classification
   (BBFC) 106
British National Party (BNP): and St
   George's Day 6–7
Buchanan, Paul 101
Bugerru (Sardinia) 17

Caesar, Julius 99
Caesarism 96, 99–101, 107
Cagliari: mass rioting (1906) 17
capitalism 30, 33, 84, 95, 102, 119, 131–2
car ownership 49
Catholic Church 45, 46, 54, 89, 124
Cavour, Count Camillo 14
Centre for Contemporary Cultural Studies (CCCS) (Birmingham) 127
Chambers, I. 117–18
Chaney, D. 87
Chirac, President 39
cinema 78, 117 *see also* films
civil society 7, 32–3, 39, 45, 48, 50, 51, 52, 77, 96
Clarke, John 96, 129, 131
class 5, 126, 127
Clockwork Orange, A 106
coercion: and consent in hegemony 49–52; shift towards in crisis 95, 97, 107
Cohen, Phil 65
common sense 4, 9, 32, 54, 123, 130; and excellence 63; and hegemony 54, 68; and intellectuals 93
Communist International (Comintern) 23
Communist Manifesto (Marx and Engels) 112
Communist Party (Italy) *see* PCI
consent 3, 47, 64, 83–4, 95; and coercion in hegemony 49–52
corporatism 45, 65
Cosmo, Umberto 18
crisis 33, 95–107; and Caesarism 96, 99–101, 107; and fictional texts 98, 105–7; organic 95, 96–8, 99, 101; and passive revolution 98–9; and *Policing the Crisis* (Hall *et al*) 96, 102–5, 107, 127, 128
Critcher, Chas 96
Croce, Benedetto 18, 19–20, 26, 27, 89, 124
cultural pessimism 76
Cultural Studies 122, 125–9
culturalism 125–6

culture 4, 27–40, 126; and Americanism–Fordism 116–19; and economic relations 4–5, 34, 39; and national-popular 36–9; and structuralism 125; *see also* popular culture
Currell, Sue 115

Daily Mirror 51
de Tocqueville, Alexis: *Democracy in America* 109
Deal, Terrence 60
Diana, Princess of Wales 101
Dickens, Charles: *Hard Times* 112
domination: and hegemony 5, 10, 41, 52
Dostoevsky 36
Douglas, Mary 64
Downey, J. 85
du Gay, Paul 59, 60, 64
Dworkin, Andrea 92

Eagleton, Terry 48, 97, 131
economic downturn 59
economic relations: and culture 4–5, 34, 39; and superstructure 28–9
economism 43, 47
education 88, 90
encoding/decoding model 127–8
Engels, Friedrich 28, 112
environmentalism 70–1
Eurocommunist movement 122
excellence, ideology of 59–64

factory councils 22, 34, 85
fascism 20, 22–3, 24, 26, 42, 96, 99, 105
feminism 92, 113–14, 130, 131
Fenton, N. 85
Fiat factory take-over (1920) 82
fictional texts: and crisis 98, 105–7
films 69; 'backlash' 98; violence and law-and-order in 106
First World War 20, 31
Fiske, John 127
fitness activities 63
folklore 36–7, 53–4

football 63; hooliganism 8, 9
force *see* coercion
Ford, Henry 109, 112
Fordism *see* Americanism–Fordism
Forgacs, David 38
Foucault, Michel 132
France: hosting of World Cup (1998) 39
French Revolution 44
Front National (FN) 39
functionalism 68

Garibaldi, Giuseppe 14
Garzia, Raffa 17
Gentile, Giovanni 19
Germino, Dante 25–6
Gilligan, Andrew 78
Gilroy, Paul 38
Gioberti, Vincenzo 44
Gledhill, Christine 78
gobalization 35, 118
good sense 54–5, 129, 130
Gramsci, Antonio: arrest of and imprisonment 24–5; death 25; early life 16–17; influences on intellectual formation 18, 19; interest in linguistics 35–6; in Moscow 23; personality and private life 16, 23, 24; political activism and Communist Party involvement 21, 22, 23–5, 31; and Sardism 17–18, 34; in Turin 16, 17–18
Gramsci, Delio (son) 24
Gramsci, Francesco (father) 16
Gramsci, Gennaro (brother) 16, 17
Gramsci, Giulia (wife) 23, 24, 25, 112
Gramsci, Giuliano (son) 25
Gray, Ann 62
Great Depression 110

Hall, Stuart 57–8, 76, 85, 96, 127, 128
Hardt, Michael 132
healthy lifestyle: and ideology of excellence 62–3
Hebdige, Dick 66–7, 118, 127, 132

hegemony 10, 36, 41–79, 122, 124, 126, 130; challenging of authority by subaltern groups 47, 53; coercion and consent 49–52; and common sense 54, 68; and domination 5, 10, 41, 52; and excellence 59–64; expansive 52–3, 130; and good sense 54–5; institutional 48, 76–9; limited 52–3; as an ongoing form of negotiation 4, 45, 48, 55, 127; role of texts in dominant bloc 70–2; roots of 42–5; textual negotiation and resistance 72–6; use of by Gramsci as tool for historical and political analysis 45–9; and youth subcultures 64–8
Higson, Andrew 75
historical bloc, notion of 34
historicism 122–5
Hollows, J. 87
Hollywood 117
Holub, Renata 132
hooliganism, football 8, 9
Horkheimer, Max 48
Howell, Jeremy 63, 64
Hunt, Leon 106
Hurd, Geoff 74

idealism 28, 124, 125
idealist realism 19–20
identity 58; and excellence 58–64
ideology 27, 28
Il Grido del Popolo 21
imperialism 38
Ingham, Alan 63, 64
institutional hegemony 48, 76–9
institutions 81; identities produced through relationships with 58; and intellectuals 81
intellectuals 10, 15, 37, 55, 78, 81–93, 111; assimilation of traditional 88–9; collective 82; and common sense 93; expansion 85–6; and Internet 85; organic 10, 83, 84–7, 88, 89, 90, 93; and popular culture and common sense

90–3; and pornography 91–3; traditional 10, 83, 87–90, 93, 124
interest groups 58
Iraq war (2003) 46, 77
Israeli–Palestine conflict 85
Italian Communist Party *see* PCI
Italian Socialist Party *see* PSI
Italy: film industry 118; and First World War 20; growth of fascism 20–1; language 35, 38; Risorgimento 14–15, 16, 98–9; South–North relations 17, 18, 34–5; *trasformismo* 15, 16, 26, 52, 99

Jacobinism 44
Japan 59
jazz 117
Jefferson, Tony 96, 127

Kelly, Dr David 77, 78, 79
Kennedy, Allan 60

Labriola, Antonio 19
Lacan, Jacques 125
Laclau, Ernesto and Mouffe, Chantal: *Hegemony and Socialist Strategy* 129–32
'lads' 67–8
Landy, Marcia 132
Lawner, Lynne 18
leadership 45–6, 48, 50, 61, 67; and Caesarism 96, 99–101, 107
learning 88
Left 129, 130
Lenin, Vladimir 19, 21, 26, 42–4, 83, 90
Lévi-Strauss, Claude 125
Lewis, Sinclair: *Babbitt* 114
linguistics 35–6
literature 36, 69, 105, 116
Livingstone, Ken 8
Livingstone, Sonia 3
'Livorno split' 22, 23
Lo Piparo, Franco 35
Logan, Steven 119
Lukács, Georg 124

Lunt, Peter 3

'McDonaldization' 119
McDonald's 78
Machiavelli, Niccolò 19, 49–50; *The Prince* 49–50, 101
Mackinnon, Catherine 92
'man of destiny' *see* Caesarism
management 60, 61
Marx, Karl 18, 19, 27–8, 33; *Communist Manifesto* 112; *The Eighteenth Brumaire of Louis Bonaparte* 100; *The German Ideology* 28; and ideology 28, 32; and superstructure 28–30
Marxism 27, 83, 123–4, 130, 132, 133
Marxism Today (journal) 129
Mazzini, Giuseppe 14
Mercer, Colin 5, 62–3
Mexican Zapatistas 85
Mezzogiorno 16, 17, 34, 47
military elites 101
Millions Like Us 73–5
mod subculture 66
Moderate Party 14, 15, 52, 98
Mondovino 119
Moores, Shaun 79, 87
morality 114
Morley, David 127–8
Morton, Adam 123
Mouffe, Chantal 129–30
'mugging' panic (1970s) 102, 104
Murdoch, Rupert 79
Mussolini, Benito 20, 22, 23, 24, 89, 96, 99, 105

Naples 111
Napoleon III, Emperor 100
national liberation movements 88
national-popular 7, 35, 36–9, 40, 105; criticisms of 37–9; and Southern Question 34–6; and Thatcherism 128
nationalism 88
nationhood 38

negotiation, textual 69, 72–5
Negri, Antonio 132
neogrammaticists 35
neolinguistics 35
New Deal 99
New Right ideology 129
new social movements 122, 129–33
New Times discourse 129
News Corporation 79
Nixon, Sean 86

Observer 51
On Deadly Ground 70–1
opera 36
Ordine Nuovo, L' (The New Order) 21
organic crisis 95, 96–8, 99, 101
organic intellectuals 10, 83, 84–7, 88, 89, 90, 93
O'Shea, Alan 117

'parasitic' class: and Americanism 110–11
passive revolution 96, 98–9; Americanism as form of 110
'passive sedementations' 110–11
PCI (Italian Communist Party) 18, 22, 23–4, 30, 49
peasantry 45, 46
petite bourgeoisie 86–7, 114, 115
'philosophy of praxis' 55
Pitkin, Professor Walter B.: *Life Begins at Forty* 115
Policing the Crisis (Hall *et al*) 96, 102–5, 107, 127, 128
political correctness (PC) 8–9
political parties 47, 97, 100
political society 50, 52, 77
popular culture 37, 98, 116, 122, 126; and Americanism 110; and intellectuals 90–3
pornography 91–3
positivism 18
post-Fordism 118, 132
post-structuralism 132
Poulantzas, Nicos 123–4
Powell, Enoch 103–4
power 3–5

Prison Notebooks, The (Gramsci) 25–6, 44, 49, 50, 82, 87, 98, 115, 116, 132
Probyn, Elspeth 78
Prohibition 113
PSI (Italian Socialist Party) 18, 22, 31
psychoanalysis 115

Ransome, P. 31
rap 75–6
regulation theory 121
religious leaders 90
representation: and hegemony 67–76; of crisis 105-7
resistance: and texts 75–6
revolution, passive *see* passive revolution
revolutionary action: Gramsci on 30–1
Risorgimento ('the Resurgence') 14–15, 16, 98–9
Ritzer, G. 119
Roberts, Brian 96
Robespierre, Maximillen 44
Roosevelt, Franklin D. 99
Rose, Tricia: *Black Noise* 75–6
Ross, Andrew 70–1, 92–3; *No Respect* 91
Russia 42
Russian intelligentsia 83
Russian Revolution 21, 30, 31

St George's Day (case study) 5–10
Salaman, Graeme 59, 60, 61
Salvemini, Gaetano 17
Sardinia 16–17
Sardism 17–18, 34
Saturday Night and Sunday Morning 117
Saussure, Ferdinand de 125
Schucht, Giulia 23
Second World War 74
self-help books 115
sexuality 114
Shakespeare, William 36
Simon, Roger 52–3
Sinclair, Upton: *The Jungle* 112
slavery 29

socialism 46–7, 82, 83, 122, 131, 132
Socialist Youth Organization 18
Southern Question 35, 37, 45, 46
'spaghetti westerns' 118
Spirit 19
sport 63
Sraffa, Piero 25
Stalin, Josef 23, 24
Straw Dogs 106
Strinati, Dominic 79
structuralism 125, 126
subcultures, youth 64–8
Sue, Eugene: The Mysteries of Paris 105
superstructure 27, 28–30, 31, 32, 33–4
Sweeney, The 106–7
symbolic violence 52

Tasca, Angelo 18
Taylor, Frederick 109
Taylorism 109, 112
television 127–8
Terracini, Umberto 18
Texier, Jacques 34
texts 5, 52, 58, 69–70, 98; crisis and fictional 98, 105–7; and negotiation 69, 72–5; and resistance 75–6; role in dominant bloc 70–2
Thatcher, Margaret 128
Thatcherism 128, 129, 131
Thompson, E.P. 125
Togliatti, Palmiro 18, 24
Tolstoy 36
Trading Places 73
trasformismo 15, 16, 26, 52, 99
Turin 16, 17–18; factory councils 22, 34, 85

Urbinati, Nadia 36

Verdi, Giuseppe 36
vocational schools 88
Volstead Act (1920) 11

Wall Street Crash (1929) 110
'War on Drugs' 98
war of manoeuvre 31, 101
war of position 31, 45, 46, 51, 101
Watson, Tom 6
welfare states 99
Wild One, The 117–18
Williams, Raymond 4, 74, 125
Williamson, Judith 72–3
Willis, Paul 66, 67–8; Learning to Labour 67–8, 127
Wilmott, Hugh 61
Wilson, Harold 102
Women in Management 62, 64
Woollacott, Janet 71, 72
Workers' revolts 30, 42
working class 129; alliances with other subordinate groups 42, 45; and Americanism–Fordism 110, 112–16, 120; cuture 67–8; Lenin on 43; and organic intellectuals 83, 84–7
Working Girl 73
working-class movement: in Britain 52–3

youth subcultures 64–8
'yuppie' 87

Zidane, Zinedine 39

THE NEW CRITICAL IDIOM

Series Editor: John Drakakis, University of Stirling

The New Critical Idiom is an invaluable series of introductory guides to today's critical terminology. Each book:

- provides a handy, explanatory guide to the use (and abuse) of the term
- offers an original and distinctive overview by a leading literary and cultural critic
- relates the term to the larger field of cultural representation

With a strong emphasis on clarity, lively debate and the widest possible breadth of examples, *The New Critical Idiom* is an indispensable approach to key topics in literary studies.

'*The New Critical Idiom* is a constant resource – essential reading for all students.'
Tom Paulin, University of Oxford

'Easily the most informative and wide-ranging series of its kind, so packed with bright ideas that it has become an indispensable resource for students of literature.'
Terry Eagleton, University of Manchester

For further information on individual books in the series, visit:
www.routledge.com/literature/nci

The Routledge Dictionary of Literary Terms
Peter Childs and Roger Fowler

The Routledge Dictionary of Literary Terms is a twenty-first century update of Roger Fowler's seminal *Dictionary of Modern Critical Terms*. Bringing together original entries written by such celebrated theorists as Terry Eagleton and Malcolm Bradbury with new definitions of current terms and controversies, this is the essential reference book for students of literature at all levels. This book includes:

- New definitions of contemporary critical issues such as 'Cybercriticism' and 'Globalization'.

- An exhaustive range of entries, covering numerous aspects to such topics as genre, form, cultural theory and literary technique.

- Complete coverage of traditional and radical approaches to the study and production of literature.

- Thorough accounts of critical terminology and analyses of key academic debates.

- Full cross-referencing throughout and suggestions for further reading.

ISBN10: 0-415-36117-6 (hbk)
ISBN10: 0-415-34017-9 (pbk)

ISBN13: 978-0-415-36117-0 (hbk)
ISBN13: 978-0-415-34017-5 (pbk)

Available at all good bookshops
For ordering and further information please visit
www.routledge.com